LIVING MACHINES

E. MICHAEL JONES

Living Machines

*Bauhaus Architecture
as Sexual Ideology*

IGNATIUS PRESS   SAN FRANCISCO

Cover design by Roxanne Mei Lum
Cover photo by E. M. Jones: Farnsworth House, Plano, Illinois

CONTENTS

LIST OF ILLUSTRATIONS

LIVING MACHINES

Figure 1. Walter Gropius on the Western Front, 1916

Chapter 1

FRANCE

June 1918

It was a suffocatingly hot day in June of 1918, and the Wandsbeker Hussars were now quartered in a French village on the Soissons–Rheims Line that had lost its strategic significance. For the moment, the town was simply a place to rest, away from the heat and the dust and the smell of freshly detonated explosives and the dead. In the distance one could still hear artillery fire. The town hall must have been a pleasant place at one time. In spite of all the broken implements of war that had piled up in its courtyard, there were still vines growing around the doors and windows in the stucco façade of a building that was typically European, typically French (fig. 2). The stucco-covered masonry walls did a good job of keeping out the heat and cold and were surmounted by a steeply pitched tile roof, punctuated by an eye-like window here and there. It was architecture in the vernacular style. The building was a meditation on the idea of home seen through the lens of a French culture that had been permeated by centuries of Christianity. The building was an enculturation of the values that France held dear. It provided, as buildings like this were supposed to do, shelter from the elements, privacy, a place to rest, and, now, a place to recover from a war that had already gone on too long and—something that no one could know then—would only be a prelude to a more terrible war twenty-one years later.

The house-like building that quartered the Hussars was everything that the war was not. It antedated the machine age in both style and construction. Then, in a split second, it succumbed to that age as well. A misdirected artillery shell scored a direct hit, landing on the building, which in turn landed on the Hussars, instantly killing all but one of them, a handsome and much-decorated thirty-five-year-old architect by the name of Walter Gropius. When the building fell on Gropius, it pushed his head up next to a still-functioning chimney, and as a result his life was saved. For two days and two nights Gropius lay under the rubble in a semi-conscious state. He had plenty of time to think about the fate of the West as epitomized by the collapse of its architecture—literally over his head—but he

Figure 2. Headquarters of the Wandsbeker Hussars, June 1918

Figure 3. Walter Gropius (middle) wearing the Iron Cross, second class, reviewing the troops, September 1914

related later that he spent the moments in which he was conscious thinking about his family instead.

The Great War was almost over, although it did not seem that way to the Germans. In the front near the Marne, the Wandsbeker Hussars were involved in a counteroffensive that had taken Foch by surprise. The Germans were about to lose a war of attrition, but Walter Gropius, who was about to win the Iron Cross, first class, gave no signs of feeling defeated. True, his letters to his mother were filled with concern about the situation in Vienna, where his wife and daughter were having difficulty finding enough to eat, but he had grown used to privation during the past four years.

"We're doing well", he wrote to his mother after describing the "indescribable" barrage of April 17.[1] "Sleep has become a luxury; we eat day or night when we get the chance, whatever we can manage. In the immediate future I'm hoping to get leave, if we achieve our objectives here. We can be happy: it's not the last [battle] but we've taken a giant step forward" (178).

Gropius had other reasons to be happy, as well. Not only was the war winding down (even if the outcome was in doubt, the fact that it was ending was not), he was also receiving job offers for civilian life. During the war years he received three separate offers to become director of schools of architecture in Germany, but Gropius was careful to take his time. In addition to being the architect who would design what was eventually to be seen as the first modern building—the Fagus shoe factory in Allfeld an der Leine—Gropius was interested in new forms of education as well—taking art and architecture, on the one hand, and machine technology, on the other, and creating a new era of mutual cooperation. Artisans who had been marginalized by the techniques of mass production would now join forces with their erstwhile oppressors in a marriage of convenience to both. The artisans would now design objects—beautiful everyday objects like chairs and electrical appliances—that could be mass-produced. Gropius' previous employer in Berlin, Peter Behrens, had shown the way by becoming the man responsible for design at AEG, the German electrical company. Behrens designed everything from the massive *Turbinenhalle* to the company's stationery, and Gropius was duly impressed. The capitalist and the artisan—the architect and the artist included—would join hands and produce good-looking, high-quality products that would catapult German industry into the forefront of world markets.

Now, with the end of the war, the idea could be institutionalized in the

[1] Reginald R. Isaacs, *Walter Gropius: Der Mensch und sein Werk* (Berlin: Gebr. Mann Verlag, 1983), p. 178. All translations from the German from Isaacs and throughout are my own. (Subsequent numbers in parentheses in text refer to Isaacs' book.)

educational system too. Instead of simply designing things himself, Gropius
would create a curriculum for design, which would make the synthesis of
craft and machinery a possibility for the entire German nation—in fact, for
the entire world, if it chose to go to school in Germany. The name by
which this new school of design came to be known was Bauhaus. The
name was to become a synonym for a new style of architecture that was
German in its roots but eventually—it would take another world war to
accomplish this—international in its scope. In fact, one of the names given
this style was the "International Style".

By the time it became known as a style, the architecture associated with
Bauhaus and Gropius had been reduced to something of a formula: flat
roofs, horizontal windows, non-load-bearing walls, and pilings to lift the
building above the earth. Le Corbusier, who followed Gropius into Peter
Behrens' office in the early teens of this century, wrote the formula as
early as the 1920s in France. Gropius was gone by the time Le Corbusier
showed up at the Behrens office in Berlin. It wasn't until October 1923
that the two met at the Café des Deux Magots in Paris. Gropius gave Le
Corbusier photographs of American grain silos, which Le Corbusier doc-
tored slightly—the crowns had to come off the buildings—and then pub-
lished in *Vers une Nouvelle Architecture* as graphic representations of the
Industriemonumentalismus that was the inspiration of the new style of architecture taking root after the Great War.

The new style conquered the world. "The victory of the new architecture", Gropius was to write in 1953, "is a *fait accompli* in all the civilized
countries of the world" (1026). On Gropius' eighty-fifth birthday, he received a telegram from the then president of the German Federal Republic, Heinrich Luebke, which claimed: "the entire world celebrates you as
the greatest architect of our time" (1151). In its obituary of him, the *Berliner Morgenpost* called Gropius "the father of modern architecture" (1037).
Then too, there were the not-so-flattering evaluations of what Gropius
had done, the criticisms of his housing projects. The settlements that eventually came to be known as *Gropiusstadt* in Berlin and the Projects on the
South Side of Chicago were characterized as "a city without a soul" whose
overwhelming impression was one of "architectural boredom" (1085).

But whether one liked it or not, Gropius had created a style that was to
transform the skyline of virtually every major city in the world during the
years following World War II. "Is a reasonable urban development thinka-
ble", Gropius asked in 1930, "when each inhabitant lives in his own home
with garden? I don't think so." [2] On the contrary, Gropius was to add in

---

[2] Walter Gropius, "Flach- Mittel- oder Hochbau?" October 1930, BMS Ger 208.2, Walter
Gropius Collected Papers, Houghton Library of Harvard University, p. 65.

Figure 4. Familie Gropius, 1892 (Walter, right, leaning on his mother)

an apodictic manner later on, "The only adequate method of construction for the large city is the high-rise with as much green space in the immediate vicinity as possible." [3] The way to tackle the problem of population density in the cities was to build taller buildings with bigger spaces between them. That vision of monolithic grey concrete slabs marching in

[3] Ibid., p. 5.

lockstep toward the horizon was to be this century's practical vision of the future. From Thirty-fifth and State Streets in Chicago to the suburbs of Moscow, industrial design, reinforced concrete, and the non-load-bearing wall sheathed in glass expressed the aspirations of this century in stone—or beige brick, to be more exact.

But in June of 1918, Walter Gropius had other, more pressing things to think about. Architecture, specifically the load-bearing wall, had became an immediate concern in his life. The building that lay on top of Gropius on that hot June day in France had been a modest, one-story affair that appeared to be more secure than it actually was. When the artillery shell exploded, the entire building—masonry, wooden beams, and all—collapsed. It was in many ways the architectural analogue to World War I and the collapse of the Austro-Hungarian empire and everything it stood for. Two-and-a-half days is a long time to spend inside a collapsed building. It provides the opportunity to think about architecture from a unique perspective. The load-bearing wall, for instance, takes on new significance, and the collapse of that architecture all around Gropius was for him the most visible symbol of the collapse of the German and Austrian empires and of the Christian West as well.

The cultural heritage of the West was one of the first casualties of the Great War. The house was the locus of the home; it was the primary building, sheltering the primary cell of society, the family, which was the nurturing ground of the values men held most dear. It was there that man first learned about God. It was there that he learned his native language, which the Germans refer to as the *Muttersprache*, the "mother language". It was there that he learned that his language aligned him with a particular race and state. All of the more important human activities, which give man his identity, took place in one sort of building or another, and those of most significance took place in the building known as the house.

Gropius had designed a number of conventional-looking houses before the war, but then the house-like structure in which he had sought shelter in France had literally fallen in on his head. It was both catastrophe and prelude; he would live to experience collapse of another sort soon enough. In the meantime, while waiting for German troops to dig him out, he could contemplate other things as he drifted in and out of consciousness—the sound of gunfire, for example, in a war won by the automatic weapon, which had acquired the futuristic name "machine gun". Such a banal name for something that would take so many lives. How appropriate, in a way, it was to the age.

Chapter 2

THE PROJECTS, THE SOUTH SIDE OF CHICAGO

August 1, 1990

Tawanda Williams is standing on the balcony outside her apartment. It is on the fifth floor of the first high-rise public housing building, just south of the Research Institute Tower of the Illinois Institute of Technology. It is two o'clock in the afternoon. She is wearing a long nightgown and is holding one child and has another child, a little older, at her side. She is heavy-set, twenty years old, and wears a pair of child's light-blue training pants as a hat. Two tufts of her kinky hair protrude from the leg holes of the pants. She seems surprised to see us, as well she might, for I am probably the first white man to appear there in the past thirty years. I feel a little like Stanley looking for Livingstone.

With me is Gloria Hardy, a social worker from Chicago's welfare department. She asks, "Do you live here?"

"No", says Tawanda, with an apprehensive look on her face.

Her denial strikes both me and Miss Hardy as funny. Maybe she thought we might take her for a tourist, or maybe we were supposed to think she was waiting for a bus.

Miss Hardy had explained on the way to Tawanda's apartment that not all of the public housing projects in Chicago were high-rise buildings of the sort that march off into the horizon south of the IIT campus. There are also low-rise buildings, which are virtually never vacant. They are the coveted public housing in Chicago; the high-rise projects are where you go when you have no place else. Why this difference, I wonder. Miss Hardy, who is black and has lived in the Projects herself—whose mother, in fact, still lives in the Projects—suggests that a house with a yard gives one a greater sense of possession. Even if you don't own the building, it seems as if you do. With the sense of possession comes a greater sense of responsibility, of control over one's life, and, with that, less likelihood of succumbing to the pathologies associated with the ghetto—promiscuity, despair, drinking, drugs, and so on.

Strangely enough, Walter Gropius, whose firm was responsible for designing the Projects on the South Side, had much the same views as Miss

17

Hardy's clients. In his "Statement Regarding the Desirability of Multi-Storied Buildings for Housing in City Areas of High Density", Gropius wrote:

> For many people the separate house naturally seems the welcome haven of refuge in the entanglement of a great city. Its greater seclusion, the sense of complete possession, and the direct communication with the garden are assets everyone appreciates, particularly in favor of children.[1]

Then, clearly veering from experience to the ideology of urban renewal, Gropius concluded: "All the same, the multi-storied building is a direct embodiment of the needs of our age."[2] The sense of haven, of privacy, and of protection from a hostile world: all that is to be eschewed in favor of "the needs of our age", which Gropius and the urban planners were privileged to determine a priori.

After Tawanda relaxes a bit, she admits that, as a matter of fact, she does live close by after all, in fact across the very balcony we're standing on. The balcony is an irregular L of poured concrete. It faces north, most immediately to the IIT campus directly across the street, and farther off, in the distance, to the whole mega-building skyline of downtown Chicago. One can see the black, monolithic-looking rectangle that is the Sears Tower and all the other monuments to modernity from Tawanda's balcony, which is itself a monument to modernity as well. Her building was designed by the Architects' Collaborative, the architectural firm Walter Gropius founded just after he arrived in the United States. This project, in conjunction with the Michael Reese Hospital project and the IIT campus, both designed by Mies van der Rohe, was to transform the slums of the South Side of Chicago into a prime example of the benefits of the collaboration between urban planning and Bauhaus architecture.

Roughly thirty-five years later, it is obvious that something has gone wrong somewhere. Reginald Isaacs, professor at the Harvard Architectural School and a protégé of Gropius at Harvard, expressed veiled disappointment when forced to give his final evaluation of the Projects in his biography of Gropius. But if there is disappointment here—and there is—it is the especially acute disappointment of someone who pretty much got what he wanted and then recognized too late that it wasn't what he had wanted at all. When the city of Chicago built the high-rise Projects on the South Side, Gropius got what he had been pleading for all his adult life, or at least from 1919 on when he railed against the Prussian building codes in

---

[1] Gropius, "Statement Regarding the Desirability of Multi-Storied Buildings for Housing in City Areas of High Density", BMS Ger 208 (131), Collected Papers.
[2] Ibid.

Figure 5. Gloria Hardy at the entrance to her mother's apartment in the Henry Horner Projects in Chicago

Berlin for restricting building to three or four stories. The reason for this restriction was to limit population density, but that goal could be accomplished just as easily, Gropius thought, by making the buildings taller—up to twenty stories—and putting more space between them so that the inhabitants would get their maximal share of light and fresh air. As a result, the Projects in Chicago originally had balconies with ship railings of the sort that were put around the balconies in *Weissenhofsiedlung* outside of Stuttgart just in time for one of the conventions of the German *Werkbund* in the 1920s. According to Franz Schulze's biography of Mies van der Rohe, "It is hard to defend the stunning rapidity with which most of the houses [of the *Weissenhofsiedlung*] deteriorated, within as little as one or two years. In short, Weissenhof was less a triumph of *Sachlichkeit* and functionalism than of the image . . . of modernism." [3] The South Side Projects

[3] Franz Schulze, *Mies van der Rohe: A Critical Biography* (Chicago and London: University of Chicago Press, 1985), p. 138.

are still with us—after a fashion at least. The railings are gone, though; they have been replaced by floor-to-ceiling iron mesh with holes large enough for a man to get perhaps two fingers through.

Tawanda, who has lived in the Projects all her life (her mother, age fifty-four, lives in the next building over, as do two of her sisters) remembers when the grates weren't there. She lived on the second floor then and used to swing off the balcony out over the playground, until one day she fell. She wasn't seriously injured by her fall, which is more than you can say for the people who have had things dropped on them from the upper balconies of the high-rise buildings. This, of course, is the real reason for the grates. Too many people were getting killed from things landing on them after a fifteen-story fall. Miss Hardy tells the story of a child who was hit by a manhole cover and, miraculously, survived—as a cripple, of course—for a few more years and then died. The residents of the Projects objected to the grates, claiming that they were being treated like prisoners in their own homes, but Miss Hardy's rejoinder is that, if you act like a criminal, you shouldn't complain that you end up living in a place that looks like a jail.

The door to Tawanda's apartment is wide open, facing the balcony. People move in and out in a way that bespeaks movement through a public place. One of Le Corbusier's touchstones of the modern architecture was the open floor plan, and the people passing in and out of Tawanda's apartment seem to be its sociological embodiment. The open plan was to presage new modalities in social relationships, and in the Projects on the South Side the Bauhaus crowd got their wish, although probably not in the way they intended. Instead of the free love and nudism of Weimar, Germany, practiced by the cream of Germany's social elite, we have the effect of that sort of thing on family life after three generations, as practiced, not by the Wandsbeker Hussars, but by the grandchildren of sharecroppers from Mississippi.

Clearly there is more to heaven and earth than was dreamt of in Walter Gropius' philosophy. The architects got the buildings the way they wanted them, but the sociology that flowed from the architecture was more complicated than they had expected. Instead of students improvising "musical outings in the environs of Weimar with accordion music and stamping of the feet, as well as rhythmic beating on tables and revolver shots in time to the music",[4] we have soap operas by day—on the screen of the color TV as we enter the apartment—and rap music accompanied by gunfire at night, although not necessarily in time with the music.

---

[4] Hans M. Wingler, *Das Bauhaus: 1919-1933 Weimar Dessau Berlin* (Wiesbaden: Verlag Bebr. Rasch & Co. and M. DuMont Schauberg, 1962), p. 344.

Figure 6.
The Robert Taylor Homes,
Chicago, 1990

Figure 7.
Henry Horner Projects

Figure 8.
Robert Taylor Homes

Figure 9. Gropius (wearing tanktop) with students at a beach on the Elbe River near Dessau

Tawanda's apartment is occupied by unrelated women, obliquely related children, and absent men. As we enter, one woman is standing in the kitchen corner of the living room folding laundry. She is introduced as Tawanda's friend. Some time later we learn that the child whom Tawanda is holding is this woman's child. Tawanda has two children—the older one who had been standing with her on the balcony, the younger one in the bedroom sleeping. The walls of the apartment are whitewashed cinder block, not particularly attractive as walls, but a good deal less upsetting than the hallway walls that are covered with spray-painted graffiti. Insofar as it is possible for walls to do any such thing, they positively breathe menace to the person walking between them.

The elevator was similarly covered with underclass hieroglyphics, the names of gang members, written by people with a desire to leave some mark on the smooth surface of anonymity with a can of spray paint. When I had asked what the intranscribable writing said, Miss Hardy replied, "Oh, you know, the usual, 'Peace', 'Love', and that sort of thing". We had gotten on the elevator with a black man who seemed mildly uninterested in the article I planned to write, but polite. When we reached the third floor, the elevator door would not open. When we reached the

fifth floor, it again seemed as if it wouldn't open; but we forced it open
and got out anyway.

Tawanda likes the apartment well enough—it is hers now, as opposed
to her mother's. But then again, as she has lived in the Project for her entire life, she doesn't have much basis for comparison. If she had one wish,
though, it is that the gunfire would stop.

While making the arrangements to go through the Projects, Miss Hardy
had told me that 10:30 A.M. would be too early to arrive, because no one
would be up yet; on the other hand, one would not want to get there
later in the day, because that's when the gunfire starts. The day's activities
follow the trajectory of intoxication. In the morning, people are sleeping it
off; in the afternoon, they're just getting started again. By the evening,
they've become intoxicated enough to get violent, and the method of ex-
pressing one's violent feelings here is gunfire, frequently from automatic
weapons, more portable versions of the machine gun.

"How recently was there shooting?" I ask Tawanda.

"Last night I could hear it."

"That's pretty recent", I say, and Miss Hardy chuckles.

Following the laws of motion fairly uncritically, bullets will continue on
if they don't hit what they are aimed at. One of the guards at IIT had
been killed recently by a stray bullet from across the street. The bullet left
the Projects, crossed the street, went through one of the ubiquitous plate-
glass windows so beloved of the Bauhaus school of architecture, and struck
a security guard. So much for openness to the external world. "The dwelling house", Gropius wrote in 1937, just around the time he arrived in the
United States to become head of the school of architecture at Harvard,

> should no longer resemble something like a fortress, like a monument with
> walls of mediaeval thickness and an expensive front intended for showy rep-
> resentation. Instead, it is to be of light construction, full of bright daylight
> and sunshine, alterable, time-saving, economical, and useful in the last de-
> gree to its occupants, whose life functions it is intended to serve.[5]

Judging from the behavior of the inhabitants of the Projects on the
South Side, a fortress might not be such a bad idea after all. It is clear that
it would have served the life functions of the security guard at IIT much
better than plate glass. In light of the actual behavior of the people who
live there, it's hard to think of an architecture more wildly inappropriate
to its time and place. Just as the social climate was reverting to the rule of
the jungle, Mies van der Rohe and Gropius opened vast expanses of those

[5] Gropius, "Changes in the Structure of the Family and Modern Housing", 1937, BMS Ger
208 (20), Collected Papers, p. 14.

Figure 10. Lobby, Carmen Hall, Illinois Institute of Technology

Figure 11. Façade, Henry Horner Homes

non-load-bearing walls to the most vulnerable sheets of plate glass. And a hail of bullets is the inhabitants' response. Or better: the hail of bullets was human nature's response to the utopianism of modern architecture.

As we stand talking, a man makes his appearance in the apartment. He is wearing an expensive-looking jogging suit, a baseball cap, and a gold chain, and he has a beeper on his belt. No, he is not an intern who wandered down from Michael Reese Hospital. The beeper, Miss Hardy tells me, is for making drug deals. She suspects that he is the father of one of the children, but he doesn't stick around long enough to talk about it. Beepers, according to Miss Hardy, have become one of the more desired consumer items in the Projects. The underclass has an affinity for status symbols. The rap groups wear Mercedes-Benz stars on the gold chains around their necks. And the drug dealers all want beepers, because they like to feel they are important businessmen ready to close a big deal. Anybody who can get called out of the room on business must be an important person.

So Tawanda wouldn't mind the Projects so much if it weren't for the gunfire. She tells us her mother feels the same way. The Projects, she feels, aren't a bad place to live, at least as far as the alternatives go. The alternative in this instance is Mississippi. Her mother had come up from Mississippi, where she used to pick cotton on a farm. According to Tawanda, she likes the Projects better than picking cotton. When Tawanda's uncles come up from the South, they stay in the Projects with them. They like Chicago because of the shopping. There is lots of stuff one can buy here that isn't available in Mississippi.

The Projects are, in effect, the place where Mississippi met the modern age. They are the place where Tawanda's mother met Walter Gropius and the decadence of the Weimar Republic expressed in concrete, steel, and glass. Or rather, they are the place where Tawanda's grandfather met the modern age. I have seen the phenomenon before. In Berlin in the seventies, I saw Arabs who had been completely undone by the liberal West, wasted by the unlimited freedom to drink and fornicate. The Arabs when confronted with the Great Satan more often than not slipped back into a fundamentalist rejection of everything Western. One can see it to a certain extent also in Poland, where modernity arrived in communist form, but with the same sort of buildings, designed by the same Bauhauslers in exile. Nowa Huta is virtually the same as the South Side of Chicago from an architectural point of view. Substance abuse is a big problem in both places, although the abused substance in Nowa Huta is vodka, not cocaine.

The difference is that in Poland the rationalist, modernist view of life— as epitomized in those soulless, high-rise apartment buildings—was im-

posed from without by the conquering Russian army and never internal-
ized as such by the people. The blacks from Mississippi weren't as lucky.
Intuitively, at least, they didn't know what those modern buildings meant
in the way that the Poles did. As a result, they were much more success-
fully colonized than the Poles were. The Poles, after all, had a thousand
years of Catholic culture working for them. When it came to building a
church in Nowa Huta, the communists refused, but the man who was to
become pope insisted, and in the end the communists backed down. The
church was built in Nowa Huta, right in the middle of all the ugly Bauhaus *Kultur-Bolschewismus* in cement.

A church, of course, was not part of Gropius' plan for the Projects on
the South Side of Chicago. The closest one comes to a church planned for
the area is the Robert F. Carr Memorial Chapel of St. Savior (fig. 12, 13),
a hilarious little box of beige brick and plate glass on the campus of IIT.
From the back, which is identical with its front, it looks like a structure to
house high-voltage machinery. The back door, which is identical in every
respect to the front door, faces the campus and is locked. Going around to
the other side of the building, I found the front door open and the back
door hidden behind a curtain that provides the backdrop to the chapel's
altar and tabernacle. Evidently it is a Catholic chapel—there are felt wall
hangings in evidence—but for the moment it is occupied by a group of
Muslims who have spread out their prayer rug on the floor and are bow-
ing to Mecca with their backs to the altar. It is difficult, however, to get
upset about the desecration of a Bauhaus chapel, if indeed that was what
was going on. From an architectural point of view, the building no more
resembles a mosque than it does a church. It's a bit like seeing Moonies
selling plastic flowers in an airport terminal.

The city planners in the United States were much more ruthless in ex-
cluding God from public life than their counterparts in communist Poland,
and the resistance among the blacks to Godless materialism was desultory
at best. The black man who came up from Mississippi, with perhaps a ten-
uous grasp of Protestant religion and its redaction of Christian sexual morality, found himself embraced by the modern socialist welfare state with
its dual animus against God and the family. He was not equal to the task.
Within the course of three generations in Chicago, the black family was
destroyed by the defection of the black male.

The slide into the cocaine-beeper-Uzi culture that is now regnant in
the Projects began when the black man from Mississippi got cut off from
his Christian roots by trying to live *Weimar Republik* values in Bauhaus
buildings. Possibly, it might have worked for a while with aristocratic
Prussians like Walter Gropius—but only for a while, as the decline of aris-

*Figure 12. The Robert F. Carr Memorial Chapel of St. Savior,
Illinois Institute of Technology*

Figure 13. Carr Chapel interior

tocratic English families like the Stracheys and the Stephens seems to show. For those with less cultural patrimony, the plummet into the underclass can happen virtually overnight.

The elevator that brought us up to the fifth floor of Tawanda's project building would not take us down again. The elevator's outside door can be opened only from the inside—either that, or we broke it for good when we forcibly got out of it when we arrived. So we had to go down the stairs, a prospect that didn't appeal to Miss Hardy.

The doorless, graffiti-covered stairwell exudes menace. The turns are all blind; the "chaste" (a favorite word of the Bauhaus apologists) geometry of the modern building is covered with the palimpsest of underclass rage and despair. One doesn't know whether one's being a white man will provoke an attack or whether the same type of mayhem will be accomplished by the impersonal agency of a stray bullet ricocheting off one plane of concrete after another until it finally comes to rest in a vital organ.

We reach the exit without incident. Actually the exit is a ramp reminiscent of an Interstate on-ramp or Le Corbusier's Carpenter Hall at Harvard. Ramps are a nice, gradual way to get from one level to another, but they kill space with a vengeance. On the way in, Miss Hardy had pointed out the mutilated playground equipment—swing sets without chains. The chains had been cut down because the children couldn't learn how to share them with each other. So now no one swings. It is just one more failed technological solution to a human problem. On the way out, Miss Hardy points out a young black man walking down the street, one hand a holding a bottle wrapped in a paper bag. He is already drunk. "By this evening he'll probably be shooting somebody", she says. The rage, she says, comes from their family lives—which, in the context of the South Side Projects, means it comes from how their mothers have treated them.

The black rage in the underclass, according to Miss Hardy, stems from the way black children are victimized in the nonexistent black "family". "All of these people", she says, referring to the young man with the bottle in his hand, "come from single-parent homes. They don't have any real male role models. The mothers normally date different men. Usually they don't go to church. They have children early in life, and the children aren't taken care of. They're abused. They're molested by the mothers' boyfriends if they're girls. Then anger is built in from being brought up in that type of lifestyle. When it comes to eating, the boyfriends usually get the better food from the food stamps that the mothers bring home. The usual type of insult is something having to do with the person's mother: 'Your mother drinks'. They don't insult the fathers because they don't know who their fathers are. Some of the women don't know who the fathers of their children are, either."

The rage against authority in the black underclass comes from the experience of failed parenthood. All children are vulnerable; all children are at least intuitively aware of the protection they need. When they don't get it, especially when they are molested sexually—a not uncommon phenomenon in the Projects, according to Miss Hardy—they become enraged at authority and the institutions that have let them down. And, of course, the primary institution that has let them down is their own family.

Miss Hardy tells the story of one twelve-year-old girl who had become pregnant by her mother's boyfriend. When she finally told her mother, the mother responded by stabbing the girl to death with a pair of scissors. Family pathology is hard to take. Not even reinforced concrete can contain it.

Figure 14. Walter Gropius, 1904, wearing the uniform
of the Wandsbeker Hussars

Chapter 3

SEMMERING, AUSTRIA

July 28, 1918

After his two-day-long meditation on the cultural significance of vernacular architecture and the load-bearing walls that weren't bearing their
loads—held at the bottom of a heap of rubble in northeastern France—
Walter Gropius was dug up, dusted off, and sent to Vienna to recuperate.
It was a stroke of good fortune because his wife, Alma, and two-year-old
daughter, Manon (known as Mutzi), were in Vienna, too. His wife, in
fact, was a native, a leading socialite (her salon was to become the meeting
place for the Austrian elite), and was once known as the prettiest girl in
Vienna. The daughter of the Viennese painter Emil Schindler, Alma had
caught the eye of the famous composer Gustav Mahler when she was still
a teenager. When she was twenty years old and he almost twice her age,
they married; and in the course of the next few years, she bore him one
child, a girl named Anna, while Mahler completed the crowning works of
his musical career.

Then, in 1910, while still married to Mahler, Alma caught the eye of
Walter Gropius, the handsome young architect from Berlin, while both
were at Tobelbad, a small sanatorium in the Tyrol near Toblach. On June
4, 1910, the twenty-seven-year-old architect was introduced to the thirty-
one-year-old wife of the famous composer by a doctor who was treating
both of them; then after the evening meal and a little walk, the two of
them sat by a small stream near the sanatorium and there, in the moon-
light, talked until the wee small hours of the morning. It was, as the saying
goes, love at first sight. An affair ensued.

Gropius, then a rising young star in architecture and industrial design in
Germany, was so smitten with Frau Mahler and emboldened by his own
recent successes that he felt he could force the issue. He wrote a letter to
Mahler in which he asked for his wife's hand. It was a severe blow for the
older composer, who was already seriously ill and had only a little more
than a year left to live. As one can imagine, his wife's infidelity affected
Mahler deeply—deeply enough to merit a consultation with the Viennese
doctor Sigmund Freud while both of them were in the Dutch town of

Leiden. Mahler was, of course, sensitive to the difference in age between himself and his wife and to the fact that he was not particularly robust in health. But he was unwilling to let the issue continue unaddressed, behind his back.

Neither, of course, was Gropius. He returned to Toblach. And as the Mahlers were driving through the town, they spied the young architect "hiding under a bridge", as Alma was to say later in her memoirs. The scene reminded Mahler of Walther von Stoltzing in Wagner's *Meistersinger von Nürenberg*. However, Mahler was determined to force the issue every bit as much as Gropius was. He sought out the young architect, brought him into his home, and put the issue to his wife: she could either stay or go. The choice was hers.

Alma decided in a way that was typical for her. She chose to remain with her husband and sent the young architect away. However, she continued to remain in contact with him, and the affair continued throughout the last year of Gustav Mahler's life. By the beginning of September 1910, she was signing her letters to Walter "*Dein Weib*" (Your wife).

Alma Mahler was, by all accounts, a passionate woman. Full-figured and not unpleasant to look at, she was also hard of hearing. As a result, she had a way of fixing her gaze intently on those to whom she was speaking—something that had an especially seductive effect on the men she met. She could also write torrid love letters and did so on a regular basis to the twenty-seven-year-old Walter Gropius during the last year of her husband's life. "Mein Walter," she wrote on September 19, 1910, "I want to have your baby, and I'll cherish it and care for it until the day appears on which we can sink smilingly into each other's arms—without regrets, full of security and peace" (103). "When will the time come", she wrote earlier that same month, "when you'll be lying naked on my body, when nothing can come between us, except perhaps sleep? . . . I know that I am living only for the time when I can become completely yours" (103).

Alma's letters were titillating, and their effect on the architect was predictable. He chased her from one end of Europe to another, and the letters of both were full of the clandestine arrangements necessary to avoid the watchful eye of Alma's only-too-suspecting husband. Thus there was one tryst at the Hotel Regina in Munich, to take place while Gustav was busy practicing with the Munich Philharmonic. Then, faced with an extended absence, because Mahler had taken the position of conductor of the Metropolitan Opera in New York, the two lovers arranged for a meeting in a sleeping compartment on the Orient Express. Mahler had business to take care of in Paris, so his wife would proceed from Vienna to Paris without

him; then the two of them would embark from Le Havre to New York
for the winter season at the Metropolitan.

"Our rendezvous", Alma wrote to Gropius on October 12, 1910,
"would best take place in Munich. I'll be leaving [Vienna] on October 14
at 11:55 in the morning on the Orient Express. My bed is number 13 in
the second sleeping car. I have been in the city and so don't know your
answer. This letter is a shot in the dark, but one full of hope" (104).

"I would advise you (if you come)", Alma continues, getting back to
the business at hand, "to reserve your sleeping compartment ticket from
Berlin under the name of Walter Grote—since G[ustav] is coming two
days later and may have a look at the list. Let me know as soon as
possible" (104).

Sure enough, Gropius was waiting on the train platform in Munich as
the Orient Express rolled in from Vienna on its way to Paris. According to
Gropius' biographer, the two adulterers "spent the fleeting hours on the
trip to Paris full of rapture, to which were added several secret trysts in the
next few days in Paris" (104). Then Alma and her dying husband set off
for New York, and Gropius went back to his architectural work in Berlin.
As part of the building trade show in Cologne in 1914, Gropius designed a
railway sleeping compartment for the German Imperial Railway (fig. 17).
One of the partitions was designed in accordion style so that there was
more room in front of the sink in the compartment. In his account of designing the sleeping compartment, Gropius says nothing about his own experiences on the Orient Express with Alma Mahler and what influence
they may have had on him. Gropius is also unable to say whether the Imperial Railway made use of his design or any part of it because, after the
trade show in Cologne, the First World War broke out.

In late 1910, however, Gropius had more important tasks before him.
Just after leaving the architectural offices of Peter Behrens and founding
his own firm, Gropius landed the contact for the building that was to go
down in history as the first "modern" building. It was the famous *Faguswerk*, and with its construction the rhetoric of modern architecture was es-
tablished in practice.

In discussing the ideology that modern architecture was to become,
one must make a distinction between the elements that composed it, its
"rhetoric", and the use to which they were put, the ideology proper, the
truly modern element. So the architectural elements in the *Faguswerk*—
the non-load-bearing walls, the missing corner support, the walls of glass,
the absence of ornament, the flat roof—would have to be put to use in a
particular way before the ideology that was modern architecture could be
born. And in the period before World War I, Gropius was not willing to

take the final step from architecture to ideology. That step had to wait
for the founding of the Bauhaus School in Weimar after the war and all
that happened to him in between, especially his relations with Alma
Mahler.

The first modern building was born during the high noon of Gropius'
affair with Alma Mahler. It was a factory that was to be an exaltation of industrial values; it was not supposed to be anything but *functional*. There
were to be no cornices, no molding, no decorated façade. In short, it was
to possess nothing that would distract one from recognizing that this was a
place where people got down to business. All of this is rather unremarka-
ble in factory architecture. The real significance of the *Faguswerk* (fig. 15)
came later; its use as an agent of social change would have to wait.

The important step came not when Gropius designed the *Faguswerk*,
but when he became determined to build houses that looked like the *Faguswerk*. And that did not happen until after the War. For evidence that
Gropius was unwilling to turn what he had come up with in industrial
design into an ideology of social relations, one need only look at the
houses he designed during the same period.

Haus von Arnim in Falkenhagen (fig. 18), for example, which Gropius
built in 1911, is conventional in the best sense of the word. It holds to the
conventions of the house as practiced in Germany at the time. That is to
say, the roof is not flat, and the windows are framed in white. It looks like
a house that one could live in, which is more than one can say of the later
Bauhaus dwellings. The only indication of the influence of the *Faguswerk*
is a *wintergarten*—a greenhouse attached to one side of the house. It is, of
course, virtually all glass, with a flat roof, but surely the sort of thing one
would expect in a greenhouse. Seen in retrospect, its presence next to the
house takes on a sinister character. Like a tumor that eventually kills its
host, the glass box that began innocently enough as a place to grow plants
became the house itself. It was to take over the home; it was to become a
replacement for the home.

Even the workers' housing that Gropius designed and built in Dramburg (fig. 19) in 1912 had pitched tile roofs in the classic German style.
Just as the church was the building that came to epitomize the Gothic
style in architecture, so that every Gothic building was in effect an imitation church, workers' housing, as subsidized by the Social Democrats in
Germany in the twenties, became the apotheosis of what Bauhaus architecture stood for. Bauhaus as a full-blown architectural ideology—as opposed to an accumulation of architectural rhetoric—stood for a socialist
rearrangement of social life, as seen most specifically in a rearrangement
of the family. In 1937, Gropius was to write in "Changes in the Struc-

Figure 15. Fagus Shoe Factory (Faguswerk)

ture of the Family and Modern Housing", when the Bauhaus ideology
was complete:

> Evolution shows a progressive growth of the collectivization of what were
> formerly family functions in the spheres of authority, education and domes-
> tic economy; transferences that are naturally reflected in the type and form
> of the buildings devoted to family life. The shelter required for the now di-
> minished and otherwise transformed family unit has changed its nature in
> accordance with its changed functions. The size of the dwelling has dimin-
> ished, the mechanical labor-saving devices installed in it are continually
> increasing.[1]

In a lecture entitled "Die soziologischen Grundlagen der Minimal woh-
nung", given on October 27, 1929, Gropius gives some idea of the
"meaning" of the new architecture, at least in terms of the sociological
changes it is to bring about. He begins his talk by positing four great social
epochs in the past, "the epoch of the tribe, the epoch of the family, the
epoch of the individual, and the epoch of the future, which is to be socialistic in its orientation".[2] We now find ourselves in a transition from period three to period four. The patriarchal family is born out of the
"enslavement of woman",[3] and this patriarchy was in the ascendancy until

---

[1] Gropius, "Changes in the Structure of the Family and Modern Housing", p. 7.
[2] Gropius, "Die soziologischen Grundlagen der Minimalwohnung", BMS Ger 208.2 (48),
Collected Papers.
[3] Ibid.

Figure 16. Gropius and his daughter Manon (Mutzi), ca. 1926

Figure 17. Sleeping compartment designed by Gropius, 1914

Figure 18. Haus von Arnim in Falkenhagen, 1911

Figure 19. Haus Metzner in Dramburg, 1906. The first house Gropius designed

the dawn of the modern industrial state. Through the possibility of the domination of nature through technology, the egocentric individualism of the past will be replaced by the socialized individualism of the future. The consequence of this increase in the concept of individual rights is a decline in the influence of the family. "Step by step, the family hands over its functions to the state, and as a result the previous sociological status of the family slowly sinks in influence in society."[4] Technology plays an inevitable role in the matter. "With the increase of the means of transportation, the independence of the individual increases. As a result, family structure is loosened and its influence reduced."[5] These ideas bring with them certain consequences for architecture:

> The rented apartment replaces the inherited family house; being settled in one place is replaced by a new nomadic individualism, which is fostered by the rapid increase of mechanized means of transportation. Just as the tribe lost its land, so the family will now lose its house. The power of the cohering family retreats in favor of the state-recognized rights of the individual.[6]

This development, Gropius continues, "demonstrates a progressive socialization of the functions formerly fulfilled by the family . . . and with this development one can just now see the development of a new communitarian era that is now in the process of replacing the previous era of the individual".[7] The recognition of the "weakness of the individual household awakens in us the idea of new forms of the mega-household, which will relieve the individual woman of her household responsibilities through central organization, which will allow her to get her work done more effectively than she would be able to do through the use of her own resources."[8]

Gropius then goes on to cite statistics showing the decrease in family size and the increases in divorce, illegitimacy, and the number of people living alone. He then proposes what he claims will be an architectural solution to this problem. With the benefit of hindsight, however, one can see that it was a "solution" that only accelerated the tendencies he cited as problematic in the first place. His solution was the "small apartment", the *Minimalwohnung*, assembled like "building blocks" on top of each other, creating *Wohnbergen*, "apartment mountains" (fig. 20, 21), in which all of the necessities were taken care of in centrally organized, quasi-public facilities, along the lines of factory cafeterias.

[4] Ibid.
[5] Ibid.
[6] Ibid.
[7] Ibid.
[8] Ibid.

Figure 20. Wohnberg (Mountain for Living) by night

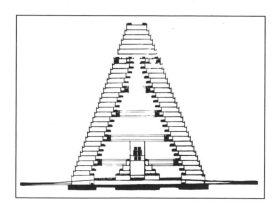

Figure 21. Wohnberg (cross-section)

To give another example of the abolition of functions formerly provided within the matrix of the family: Gropius proposed the industrialization of the hearth. Heating was to be produced in remote buildings and then piped into the apartment complexes, obviating the need for individual furnaces in the apartments.

Everything was to be rationalized according to the latest developments in technology because

> the inner structure of the industrial family is ineluctably drawn away from the one-family dwelling to the multi-story apartment building and finally to the mega-household. . . . Just as the one-family dwelling corresponds more to the needs of more well-to-do classes in society, so also does the high-rise apartment building correspond to the sociological needs of the contemporary industrial population with its symptomatic independence of the individual and the relatively early removal of children from the family. To be sure, the multi-story high-rise offers significantly more cultural advantages than its low-rise alternative.[9]

By the time the rhetoric of modern architecture had been assembled into a modern ideology—let's say by 1925—the form and the structure of the modern apartment, which was to replace the more traditional one-family dwelling as the preferred dwelling of socialist man, had become full of sociological meaning. Instead of man's home being his castle, instead of the German idea of *Gemütlichkeit* as essential to the domestic sphere, Gropius saw his architecture in increasingly mechanistic terms. The apartment was to deliver a maximal amount of "light, sunshine, air, and warmth". The home had become "a machine for living in".[10] "Architecture", Le Corbusier states in his groundbreaking *Toward a New Architecture*, "has for its first duty, in this period of renewal, that of bringing about a revision of values, a revision of the constituent elements of the house." [11]

Just as the Gothic ended up producing imitation churches at places like Oxford, Cambridge, and Yale, so the goal of the new architecture was to produce imitation factories, or the anti-house, as a way of subverting family life. As Gropius said, "The reduction in the size of the apartment as a result of the decentralization of the family is both sensible and desirable and cannot be explained away as simply the result of passing economic crises." [12] Or as Le Corbusier put it, we need to foster "the spirit of living in mass-production houses":

---

[9] Ibid.

[10] Gropius, "Wohnmaschinen", BMS Ger 208.2 (4), Collected Papers.

[11] Le Corbusier, *Towards a New Architecture* (London: The Architecture Press, 1927), p. 12.

[12] Gropius, "Die soziologischen Grundlagen der Minimalwohnung".

If we eliminate from our hearts and minds all dead concepts in regard to the house, and look at the question from a critical and objective point of view, we shall arrive at the "House-Machine", the mass-production house, healthy (and morally so too) and beautiful in the same way that the working tools and instruments that accompany our existence are beautiful.[13]

Gropius was also the source of Le Corbusier's notion of the apartment as a "machine for living in". In his talk "Wohnmaschinen", given in 1919, Gropius claimed that "only the things the engineer creates (water pipes, heating, electric light) correspond to the spiritual challenges of our age. The office of a modern factory takes on the organic form of its furniture; our apartments do not." [14] The source of the house of the future is not going to be any "sentimental hanging on to a past that is no longer alive".[15] No, Gropius said, turning his face toward America, the land of the future; the house of the future is going to be produced like the Ford automobile. Every adult will have a room of his own, "even if it's only a small one".[16]

[13] Le Corbusier, *Towards a New Architecture*, pp. 12–13.
[14] Gropius, "Wohnmaschinen", p. 4.
[15] Ibid.
[16] Ibid., p. 5.

Chapter 4

CRACOW, POLAND

April 1990

The cathedral at the center of Cracow is full on Wednesday morning; it is, of course, Holy Week, but there are no special services for Wednesday. A Mass is just finishing up at 9:30 in the morning: people are going to Communion. Not too long after that Mass is over, another one starts at the side altar of this huge, dark, brick Gothic cathedral. In the center nave there are a few chandeliers with a few dimly glowing bulbs, but for the most part the church is dark. One window off to the left, high up in the ceiling, is open, and a long beam of dust- and smoke-filled light descends diagonally to the carved, wooden choir benches off to the right. The entire back of the church is full of people in line waiting to go to confession. Maybe they're there because it's Holy Week, but then again Holy Week doesn't fill up the cathedral in South Bend on Wednesday mornings, and South Bend is not exactly an irreligious city. In Vienna the cathedral at the center of the city was full of tourists; in Cracow it is full of penitents of all ages, male and female.

The priest at the side altar says Mass facing the altar, but he says it in Polish, except for the canon, which he says in Latin. The Our Father is recited in Latin; at the kiss of peace, which is also announced in Latin, the people bow to each other politely. A huge crucifix with a realistic, bloody corpus dominates the space above the altar. Behind the altar one sees a bronze relief of a city that looks to be in flames, possibly Cracow itself. As in most churches of this sort, the verticality is striking to a twentieth-century American. This is not the church of the dropped ceiling. It is not the chapel at IIT or any of its simulacra. The pillars rise on either side of the altar and are surmounted by angels who hold spears and other such things. The architecture keeps going up and up and becomes more theologically complicated along the way. So there are lessons here in stone, just as there are in the United States.

In the United States, recent church architecture proclaims godlessness, no matter what the piety of the minister and flock says to contradict it. If there is piety in modern American churches, it is there in spite of the

41

architecture and not because of it. These squat, flat-roofed, beige-brick, warehouse-like structures—a sort of imitation of the *AEG Turbinenhalle* or the *Faguswerk*—seem to have been built with the communist revolution in mind. If the churches had to be transformed into basketball courts or airplane hangars, as happened in Albania, there wouldn't be a whole lot of cost involved. They were built to look like basketball courts to begin with. The average church built in the United States since the sixties looks like the parochial school gym set up for an assembly.

The cathedral in Cracow, on the other hand, would require a great deal of renovation to look like a basketball court. This is probably the reason why the communists in Poland never even tried. (This may also be the reason why you never hear much about Albanian basketball teams.) The church was built to be a church; it was a monument to the supernatural and not an imitation shoe factory. It evokes the supernatural in stone every bit as much as the newer churches bespeak atheism or banality. Everything that happens in the new churches suffers from the banalizing influence of factory architecture. Whereas in Cracow, one could redeem even the most pedestrian sermon by looking up at the ceiling.

It's a battle the Church lost before she began it. The Second Vatican Council occurred forty years too late or thirty years too soon. It should have been held in 1989 after socialism collapsed in the East or in 1919 when Christendom (or what was left of it) collapsed in Europe in general. Instead it arrived during the sixties, at a time when everyone still believed in the modern age; it arrived when people thought that flat roofs were practical and that Margaret Mead was an anthropologist, Sartre a philosopher, and Paul Tillich a theologian. For Catholic colleges and universities it was the high noon of Catholic inferiority complex as they rushed, lemming-like, off the high ground of the Catholic intellectual tradition, headlong into the sea of government funding. Catholic intellectuals for the most part lusted after modernity.

Openness to the age meant the uncritical adoption of ideas that were not only the antithesis of Catholicism but the antithesis of the entire culture of the West. In West Germany, for example, one can see, in a church of suitably modern stripe, a cross made of twisted automobile bumpers, and also abstract Stations of the Cross. This sort of failure was repeated on a massive scale throughout the architecture of the West. It was Catholic cultural failure on a massive scale. The Church should have held off for another thirty years. She should have waited until the modern project collapsed completely, until Brave New World-West followed Brave New World-East into the dustbin of history. Now, at least half the cat is out of the bag.

The number-four trolley car in Cracow takes you from just outside the center of town right near the train station to Nowa Huta, the Polish communist version of the worker's paradise. For three cents, it's not a bad ride. On the afternoon of Holy Thursday, the tram is jammed with people going home from work. Since Malopolska is rich in coal, someone had the idea of building a steel plant there, which of course was named after Lenin, and then, so the workers wouldn't have far to go, the communists built the workers' housing there, too. Everything was planned, except a church, which the atheists didn't think was necessary in Brave New World-East. The people, however, were of a different opinion, as was Karol Wojtyla, the archbishop of Cracow at the time, and a stand-off quickly escalated into demonstrations—after which the church was built. It looks a little like a steel plant on the top, probably intentionally so, although there is so much "steel plant" in the atmosphere that one doesn't need it in the church too.

The people in Nowa Huta live in the high-rise, socialist workers' housing that Walter Gropius thought corresponded to the needs of the decentralized family in the industrial age. Someone, however, failed to tell the Polish workers that this was the liberation from family ties they had been longing for. It was a little like Walter Gropius looking into the future and deciding that the course of evolution determined that men's feet were growing smaller all the time, and that the state shoe factory should therefore produce nothing larger than size-eight shoes. The Poles were then left with the unenviable task of getting their various-sized feet into the shoe of the future, no matter how uncomfortable they found it.

Nowa Huta is made up of boxes, box-like apartments piled on top of each other, creating very large high-rise boxes, which correspond in an almost literal way to Gropius' system of design. *Baukasten im Grossen*, it was called, which we can translate roughly as "giant building blocks". The building-block buildings are made out of reinforced concrete, which means they are gray to begin with, and they get grayer with time because of all the coal smoke pouring out of the Lenin Steel Plant—one of the world's worst polluters, according to *Rolling Stone Magazine*. The communists, who think of everything, have painted the insides of the balconies various garish colors. They also have placed pieces of equally garish corrugated plastic at various points in the architecture. The up-beat colors on the concrete walls of the apartment buildings are also grimy from the coal smoke, and the effect is about as cheering as party decorations the next morning or a plastic Santa Claus on a roof in July.

Among the symbols for the social failures of the twentieth century, the apartment-box is as appropriate as any. It captures the essence of atheistic

socialism in a way that no monument of some cement man with bulging
biceps and carrying a submachine gun can. It is a monument to man as a
packageable commodity. It was the one thing that the communist East and
the consumerist West had in common. Both civilizations wanted to put
people in boxes. The New Man was to work in a glass box during the day
and then, in the evening, go home and live in a cement box at night. The
box is virtually the same the world over. Nowa Huta is really no different
from the South Side of Chicago or Peabody Terrace at Harvard University.

The apartment-box not only looks the same the world over; it creates
the same sort of malaise in the human soul. Even the graffiti is the same.
The Polish wallwriters favor a familiar four-letter English word beginning
with *F.* Perhaps because they are writing in a foreign language, the Polish
wallwriters tend to be more legible than their counterparts in the ghettos
of New York or Chicago or Philadelphia. Perhaps it's just that the Poles
have better penmanship. No one escapes the box in the twentieth century,
especially not if you're poor and have to live on the largesse of the state, as
do some in the United States and virtually everyone in communist Poland.
Most of us have only to look at the boxes, and the poor have to live in
them, but no one escapes them.

No, let's be more precise. There are spiritual escapes, which are real,
and there are chemical escapes, which are illusory. The regnant powers in
both the East and the West frown on both. The projects have no church,
and Nowa Huta almost didn't have one, either. The blacks in the South
Side Projects smoke crack; the Poles in Nowa Huta drink vodka. Living in
one of Herr Gropius' *Wohnmaschinen* creates, it would seem, an overwhelming desire for some type of anesthetic.

There's a lot of alcoholism in the workers' paradise of Nowa Huta,
more so than in Cracow, although it's noticeable there too. I'm not talking about statistics here; I don't know if there are any statistics. I'm talking
about people staggering through the streets, hanging onto lampposts, falling down in the gutters, cutting their heads open, as one man did in front
of the Fiat 500 from which someone sells lottery tickets. Vodka is cheap,
and we're talking about places where the principal pleasures are sex and al-
cohol. Men, as St. Thomas Aquinas said, need pleasure, and if they are de-
prived of spiritual pleasures they will seek pleasures of the flesh. The
avidity with which the inhabitants of Nowa Huta and the South Side of
Chicago seek pleasures of the flesh is the best indication of the anaphrodi-
siac quality of their surroundings. We're talking here about a group of
people who have been weakened badly by a system that crushed everything that was good and virtually begged its population to get involved in

one or another form of officially sanctioned docility. To go through the motions on the job, to get drunk, to forget about God, to act as if this were all there is—the only way to deal with any and all of it was with the help of some form of narcosis. The system fostered bad habits, and then, in Poland, the system suddenly died, but bad habits have a nasty way of hanging on after the system is gone.

Chapter 5

SEMMERING, AUSTRIA

July 28, 1918

Gustav Mahler died on May 18, 1911, Walter Gropius' twenty-eighth birthday. The young architect found himself in a curious psychological situation. The way leading to the object of his desire had been cleared of its major obstacle, but Gropius found himself reluctant to claim the prize. He was feeling full of—to use a distinctly unmodern term—guilt. On September 25, 1911, Gropius wrote to Alma, complaining,

> since I left you a burning sense of shame has come over me, which forces me to avoid you. I have to get away for a while and see whether my eyes have grown blind or whether I'm really in the position, if you wish it . . . to clothe my love in the beautiful forms which were once worthy of you and which can ease the pain I inflicted on you and Gustav out of my lack of mature foresight. Today, I just don't know, and I'm depressed about myself (113).

Adultery is, after all, adultery, and Mahler's death seems to have brought home to Gropius the magnitude of the injustice he had inflicted on the famous composer. Chances are he would have experienced the same feelings if he had had an affair with the wife of the town garbage collector—from a moral perspective there is no difference. However, over the course of the affair, Gropius began to take an interest in Mahler's work, and in the course of that investigation he began to have a clearer idea of the man he had been cuckolding. In late January he wrote to Alma about having attended the performance of one of Mahler's symphonies in Berlin:

> I just got back from a performance of Gustav's Seventh [Symphony]— exhausted, torn up inside. Listen to my impressions because I feel the need inside to talk things over with you. I feel dizzy right now, like a man who has to grab ahold of something lest he get thrown off the track of his ideals like someone who enters a foreign land full of astonishment. I easily caught onto his style and complete originality again; however, in Munich at that time so many feelings of different sorts were running through my heart to prevent my mind from coming to any definite understanding. Today, how-

ever, everything was new and strange—an alien and distant Titan shook me
to my foundation, caught me up in his colossal impulse, and touched all of
the registers of my heart from the demonic all the way to the most touching
child-like simplicity. The guileless aspiration, the lonely God-seeking in this
piece touched me deeply . . ., but I am afraid of this alien strength because
my art grows in different soil. (110)

Walter Gropius came from a Prussian Protestant family which, according to his biographer, "preserved the forms" in matters religious but not
the substance: "One belonged to Church; however, it was a superficial relationship, without any interior connection" (54). In his encounter with
the music of Gustav Mahler, Gropius encountered the spiritual world as
mediated through the music of a deeply spiritual Catholic of Jewish de-
scent. Like some of the English moderns of the same period, Gropius
found it easier to step from a nominally Protestant culture into an overtly
secular one. Gropius' description of the effects of the Seventh Symphony
on him are one of the few instances in which he discusses religion at all,
and in this instance it is only to dismiss it in the end. But not without ef-
fort. He has to "grab ahold" of his secular "ideals" lest he be too touched
by all of this musical "God-seeking". In the end he retreats from the transcendent in fear; his architecture "grows in different soil". It is to be the
antithesis of the openness to the transcendent, which had characterized the
artistic tradition of the West. Mahler was no modern, and Gropius might
seduce his wife, but Gropius feared Mahler's music and what it stood for.

The adulterous relationship, which had flamed up with such passionate
intensity in the spring of 1910, was threatening to sputter and go out by
the end of 1911. In his correspondence, Gropius showed himself less dis-
posed to rush off to spend time with Alma. In November, Alma wrote
from Paris inviting him to spend some time with her at the apartment she
had just taken, but Gropius showed little inclination to go. He was suffering from an infected tooth, which had led to blood poisoning. So instead
of a replay of the tryst on the Orient Express of the previous year, Gropius
checked into a sanatorium near Dresden and hoped for a renewal of his
energies. By December he was fit enough to return to Berlin and entertain
a visit from Alma, but the meeting was a disappointment to both of them.
The relationship cooled further, and Alma was left to console herself with
a series of letters. "Are you still true to me?" she asked in a letter written
on January 15, 1912 (114); and, on January 26, she wrote again wanting to
know why he hadn't answered her letters. She was feeling abandoned and
alone.

It was a feeling Alma Mahler never let herself feel for very long. To put
it one way, she was a deeply social person at the center of the social life of

what was still the capital of the Austro-Hungarian Empire. To put it another, she was the type of woman who would love the man she was with if she couldn't be with the man she loved. In May of 1911, right around the time of the death of Gustav Mahler, Alma met the twenty-six-year-old expressionist painter Oskar Kokoschka at the house of her stepfather, Carl Moll. Before long, Alma was deeply involved in a love affair with Kokoschka, one that she neglected to mention in the letters to Gropius in which she wondered if he was remaining true to her. Alma was impressed with Kokoschka's talent but refused to marry him until he produced a "masterpiece". It is unclear whether Kokoschka ever fulfilled Alma's requirements—but, as they never married, he probably did not. However, he did do a number of works with her in mind. He painted a fresco over the fireplace in Haus Mahler, the house the composer had built for his wife and family outside Vienna. The fresco was supposed to represent a continuation of the flames in the fireplace, and there in the middle of the flames—perhaps to signify the torment the relationship with Alma meant for him—sat Kokoschka himself. On the left side of the painting there was darkness, on the right a figure of light showing with a gesture of the hand the way out of the flames. That figure, of course, was Alma.

Alma also figured in one of Kokoschka's more famous paintings. He completed *Die Windbraut* around Christmas of 1912. In it the painter and Alma are lying naked in each other's arms, surrounded by clouds. It is a heavily erotic painting. Gropius had seen Kokoschka's works during the course of 1912 at the Storm Gallery in Berlin. When, in the spring of 1913, "The Windbride" was shown as part of the *Berliner Sezession* exhibition there, Gropius attended the exhibition and saw the painting. "I know that lady," we can imagine him thinking as he contemplated Kokoschka's masterpiece, "but who is the man in bed with her?" Gropius' biographer confines himself to saying that the "picture's message was for Walter Gropius unmistakable at first sight" (115). This sort of unpleasant recognition scene was to become a not uncommon phenomenon before long. More often than not it would become associated with Alma and Haus Mahler as well. Family relations, which seem to have been unexceptional to Gropius as a child, were, beginning with his own adulterous relationship with Alma, becoming something increasingly opaque. Perhaps as a consequence, *Klarheit* (clarity) became one of Gropius' favorite words. During the war, he wrote to his mother praising Alma, who by then *was* his wife, claiming that she does everything with "clarity and perspicacity" (179). Haus Mahler, however, as the locus of Alma's far-reaching social life and love affairs, was becoming something close to the antithesis of *Klarheit* for Walter Gropius.

In many ways the house epitomized the increasingly opaque nature of Gropius' relations with Alma Mahler. Life with her was full of unpleasant little epiphanies, like seeing the *Windbraut* at an exhibition that most of Gropius' peers in Berlin would attend. Life with Alma in Haus Mahler was the architectural antithesis of the *Klarheit* that Gropius prized. The house is, to begin with, virtually all roof, a good instance of the vernacular Austrian style, suitable to bear the heavy snows that occur at that altitude in the Alps. Beyond that, the ground floor is deeply recessed beneath what is practically a vertical drop directly from the roof. The windows are small, and whatever light comes into the first-floor windows has to filter through the shadow created by this deep overhang.

Haus Mahler is currently owned by a German shipbuilding company and used as a resort for its employees; however, Anna Mahler, Alma's daughter by Gustav, gives some indication of the way it was when they lived there before World War I.

> The architecture was nothing special, but inside it was wonderful. Everything was wood paneling, and at the beginning completely without electrical lighting. You can't imagine how wonderful it was in the evenings in the room with the fireplace with just the glowing fire and all of the candles burning.[1]

Haus Mahler was, in effect, an anti-*Wohnmaschine*. It was the antithesis of the geometric spirit of rationalism that had made such an impression on factory architecture. It was, to use a German term, *gemütlich*—a typical Austrian home. With its small windows, steeply pitched roof, and lack of electricity, it was a dark and very private place. Unfortunately (and Gropius was to feel this point more acutely as time went on), privacy at home with Alma was synonymous with an uneasy feeling that something was going on behind one's back.

Seeing "The Windbride" at the *Berliner Sezession* exhibition in the spring of 1913 had the effect of terminating—at least for a while—Gropius' relationship with Alma. For one year after the show, there was not even an exchange of letters between the two. Then, in May 1914, Gropius received a letter from Alma:

> How do I live? After fighting and wandering lost—I've found my way back to myself. I am more mature, freer—of this I'm sure—of all the things that don't concern me because I've found so much in my life. I don't stand still at any milestone. If you want my friendship, you can have it. I have a deep

---

[1] Peter Stephan Jungk, *Franz Werfel: Eine Lebensgeschichte* (Frankfurt am Main: S. Fischer, 1987), p. 106.

desire to speak with you. Your likeness remains beloved and pure in me, and people who have experienced such beautiful and strange things together mustn't lose track of each other. Come, if you've got the time and if it will make you happy, come to me. It's not resignation that makes me write to you. Rather it's a brighter and more deeply clarified view of things (159).[2]

One needn't be clairvoyant to detect the sadder but wiser tone in Alma's letter. The affair with Kokoschka had run its typical fever-like course. In the winter of 1914 she became pregnant; in the spring they quarreled again, and on May 17, 1914, she went to a clinic in Vienna and aborted the child. In June, when she reestablished contact with Gropius after a year of silence, Alma's relationship with Kokoschka reached crisis stage once again. On June 28, 1914, Archduke Ferdinand and his wife were assassinated in Sarajevo, and World War I broke out. Gropius had just completed a very conventional-looking hospital in Allfeld and had also done an equally conventional number of workers' housing settlements. Their conventionality included placing a peaked roof on each building. The war put an end to his architecture for the next five years, but it hastened his reconciliation with Alma. The two were married on August 18, 1915, but not until after their renewed affair had started people talking in Berlin during the spring of that year.

As one might expect, their relationship during the war was confined to times when Gropius either had furlough or was wounded. Alma's letters during this time take on an oftentimes unpleasant and suspicious tone. After hearing of a new venereal disease making the rounds at the front, Alma insists on knowing whether Gropius has been faithful. There is no indication that he wasn't. His time was spent in being a soldier, although at one point, shortly before the birth of their daughter Manon in February 1916, he did make use of his free time to design an addition to Haus Mahler. The idea, which was to add a porch onto the house near the dining room, seemed innocent enough, but it provoked a fit of rage from Alma when he mentioned it in one of his letters. The reaction seems out of all proportion to the proposal and leads one to wonder what psychological meaning a terrace adjoining the dining room had for Alma. Or perhaps it was simply the fact that Gropius was infringing on a house that bore the name Mahler and was associated with her first husband. Either way, it couldn't have made Gropius feel very good about his relationship with his wife, already burdened by the separations and privations that war imposed. In addition, Gropius was surely aware that Alma had let Kokoschka paint

---

[2] Also see Karen Monson, *Alma Mahler: Muse to Genius* (New York: Houghton Mifflin, 1983), p. 159.

that fresco over the fireplace. Once again, Gropius had run into forces that were deeper than he was able to plumb. The terrace project was dropped, but, especially because of the insults Alma piled on him in her letter, not forgotten.

Two years later, in the summer of 1918, Gropius was back in Semmering, although not living in Haus Mahler with his wife. In January of 1918, after returning from the Italian front, Gropius learned that his wife was pregnant. In May, the building where he was staying in France took a direct hit and collapsed. On July 28, 1918, in consideration of the injuries he had suffered and the fact that his wife was facing a difficult birth—partially because of the privations of the previous winter—Gropius was transferred to the army hospital in Semmering to recuperate and take care of his wife.

Shortly after he had arrived, early in the morning of August 2, Gropius was awakened by a message from Carl Moll, Alma's stepfather. During the night Alma had started hemorrhaging, and he was requested to go to her at once. Full of foreboding, the young officer stepped out of the train station and hurried to his wife. As he left the train, Gropius was too full of concern for his wife to notice a short fat man from Prague waiting at the same station for a different train. His name was Franz Werfel. Eventually, he would become famous for writing a book called *The Song of Bernadette*, about the apparitions of the Blessed Mother in the French town of Lourdes, a book that was later made into an extremely successful motion picture starring Jennifer Jones. But that was all more than two decades in the future. Right now Werfel was involved in an affair with a married woman. The woman was pregnant and having medical problems. She had started hemorrhaging in the middle of the night. It seemed as if she might lose the baby.

Chapter 6

RASTENBURG, WOLFSSCHANZE, EAST PRUSSIA

April 14, 1990, Holy Saturday

Everyone, it seems, wants to leave some architectural legacy—Stalin no less than Hitler. But we do not often get to leave the monuments of our choice. So, for example, one of the prime monuments to the megalomania and general stupidity of Nazism is Hitler's *Wolfsschanze*, a poured-concrete Stonehenge in what used to be East Prussia and is now a part of Poland near the Russian border. "*Kwatery Hitlera*", the sign says in Polish, and as one enters the compound there is a large map describing who lived in which bunker and explaining the purpose of the other buildings. Building number two, we learn, was the *Führer*'s movie theater. The Wolf's Lair wouldn't be complete without a movie theater, now, would it? The other buildings are all virtually indistinguishable heaps of exploded concrete. All, that is, except for Hitler's bunker, which is the biggest of them all and right in the middle of the camp. It is roughly twenty-five feet high, a huge block house of reinforced concrete, its walls at least fifteen feet thick. The flat roof was covered with dirt and planted with trees and bushes, so the whole thing was nearly invisible from the air. During its heyday, the camouflage nets over the *Wolfsschanze* were changed with the seasons. Not that that mattered much, though. The bunkers were all blown up from the inside. The places for the dynamite charges were planned from the very beginning. In fact, it would have been impossible to blow the thing up from the outside, even if the Russians could have located the bunkers.

The whole complex of buildings is now covered with forest—some of it intended as camouflage, most of it just nature taking over—the thinly leaved foliage of the eastern Baltic in spring. The forest is mostly birch trees—things are starting to look Russian here—and of course we are only about ten kilometers from the Russian border. In fact, the whole complex of buildings was built as the position from which Hitler was to direct the campaign against Russia. Now Prussia is part Russia, part Poland. One wonders what Immanuel Kant would have thought of being a Russian from Kaliningrad, the name Königsberg currently goes by. There is, one

Figure 22. Hitler's Headquarters

quickly notices, virtually no contact across the border, in spite of all the propaganda about friendship with the Soviet Union and the solidarity among socialist countries. Everyone laughs at that idea now. The Poles were forced to spend twelve years in school learning a language they could already understand, but which none of them would ever use, because there was little contact between the two countries. It was a monument to socialist inefficiency in language training. In terms of cultural contact, Russia is farther away from this part of Poland than is the United States, which, as one has come to expect, dominates the popular culture of this country. So there are the usual obligatory graffiti on the bridges along the road from Ostroba to Gdansk: Metallica and Megadeath. And the people in Poland who watch television get to see *Miami Vice, Autostrada do Ni-nieba* (*Highway to Heaven*), and *North and South*, the last a series whose run threatens to be longer than the Civil War itself.

Stalin got the monuments he deserved, too. Not bunkers, but apart-ment buildings, the boxes that cover all of Eastern Europe like some loath-

some tetter. Where, I wonder as we drive though Masuria, is saturation
bombing when we really need it? Saturation bombing would have been
fine with me if it had only been used on the works and pomps of the
twentieth century. But, like the Oedipus Complex, Bauhaus architecture,
moral relativism, contraception, deficit spending, the automobile, and cubism, saturation bombing was used as the twentieth century's revenge on
the cultural legacy of the West. It was an attempt to use the power of the
West in order to destroy the West. It was just one more instance of the
parasitic nature of the modern age. Thus saturation bombing was military
cubism, a sum of destructions, as Picasso would have called it. It was an attempt to rearrange our culture according to modern principles. It came
from the same root as cubism and led to the same results. Saturation
bombing was just a more effective form of cubism. That's all.

Herr Dembrowsky and I get on famously. On the way to the horse
farm at Lyski, which is less than five kilometers from the Russian border,
we break into the chorus of "The Internationale" in German in two-part
harmony. (I heard the communist anthem only two other times during
my trip: once while Mikhail Gorbachev and friends sang it at the hundred
and twentieth anniversary of Lenin's birth, after a speech at the Bolshoi
Theater in Moscow, and once sung by a deeply deranged man sitting on
the sidewalk in front of a department store in Wroclaw. That was a good
indication of the constituency that is left to communism in Eastern
Europe.)

> Völker hört die Signale
> Auf zum letzten Gefecht
> Die Internationale
> Erkämpft das Menschenrecht.

It was good for a laugh while riding in the car, especially that bit about
fighting for the rights of man, sung with the delicious sort of irony known
only to those whose rights had been trampled on for forty-five years but
who had outlived the system that tried to do them in. The only people
who could sing it without irony now were either communist functionaries
or the certifiably insane. One of the few pleasures left to the people in this
part of the world is the general recognition that something so wrong from
the beginning had failed so utterly in the end.

Herr Dembrowsky, it turns out, had been a surveyor for the state
agency that built the apartment-boxes all over this part of Poland. I am
stunned by my good luck. Now, I tell myself, I will be able to find out
who designed all these ugly buildings. Was it Stalin? Did he invent the
apartment-box after he discovered the laws of physics, around the time,

say, that he invented the airplane and baseball? My hopes are quickly
dashed. Herr Dembrowsky doesn't know any more about the designer of
the buildings he helped build than I do. "It was architecture by photo-
copier", he says. Every building was exactly the same except for the balconies, which could be slightly rounded in one version, square in another.
Of course the balconies could also be painted different garish colors—
yellow and orange being two favorites, it seems. And, of course, each
building had a large number painted on its side to distinguish it from the
identical building next to it, so that people who were drunk could find
their way home in the night. Herr Dembrowsky himself lives in one of
the very buildings he helped spread like architectural toxic waste across the
countryside. It is, I suppose, a good instance of where the punishment fits
the crime. Perhaps life in the box can also be used in exchange for time
spent in purgatory—which may or may not be a good deal.

These boxes, in addition to being ugly, are also shoddily built. When
the temperature drops, as it tends to do in northeastern Poland in the winter, the walls crack; and then the wind coming through the walls necessitates all sorts of provisional measures, things being stuffed into cracks to
stop the drafts. And, even with all that, when the wind blows hard, the
building whistles. So who was the anonymous hero of socialist humanity
who designed these buildings? I want to know, but Herr Dembrowsky
just shrugs his shoulders and laughs.

The connection with Bauhaus is, however, quite direct, almost as direct as the connection between Walter Gropius and the South Side of
Chicago. In late January of 1933, Gropius gave a speech at Leningrad in
which he praised the Soviet Union as "up until now the only country
that has achieved the most important precondition for healthy urban renewal, namely, free land".[1] By "free land", Gropius meant the abrogation
of the right to own property, which went into effect in Russia in 1917
with the Communist Revolution. "All sensible urban planning", he continued, "must remain purely utopian as long as society permits its inhabitants to retain private property."[2] Once the ground had been cleared, so
to speak, in that regard, Gropius went on to recommend what he had
been suggesting to the Germans since 1919, that, "instead of the usual
middle-rise three- and four-story apartment buildings", the Soviets should
build ten- to twelve-story high-rise apartments.[3]

The Soviets, as a trip to Moscow will show, were only too happy to act

[1] Gropius, "Deutsche Architekturausstellung in Leningrad, 31 Januar 1933", BMS Ger 208.2
(96), Collected Papers.
[2] Ibid.
[3] Ibid.

on Gropius' suggestion. Bauhaus fit in with the communists' view of urban planning like hand in glove, not because Gropius was an active member of the Communist Party in Germany—he was not. Nor did he have to be. What he did have was a profoundly secular idea of man and of the family and of the relations between the sexes, as well as a design for buildings that embodied these ideals. That philosophy was incorporated into a style of architecture undeniably modern; it had about it the air of scientific rationality so beloved of communist ideologues. Gropius had come up with the new dwelling for the new man, and the fact that he wasn't a member of the Communist Party was irrelevant. Bauhaus was, as his contemporaries in Germany claimed, *Kulturbolschewismus*. Anyone could see that.

In July of 1933, Gropius was back in the Soviet Union, again saying much the same thing in even stronger terms. In 1952, in a speech entitled "Was erhoffen wir vom russischen Städtebau?"—he said:

> The worst hindrance [to urban planning] is the immoral right of private ownership of land. Without the liberation of the land out of this private slavery it is impossible to create a healthy, development-capable, urban re-newal that is economic in terms of society in general. Only the Soviet Union has fulfilled this most important requirement without reservation and thereby opened the way for a truly modern urban planning.[4]

Four years after he made this speech, Gropius was chairman of the archi-tecture department at Harvard. From then on, he refrained from using phrases like "the immoral right of private ownership". From then on he re-ferred frequently to "our belief in democratic government".[5] "Planning", he said in the fifties, "grows from the ground up and not from the top down by force."[6] One wonders what Stalin would have thought of these sentiments and why Gropius didn't express them when he was in Leningrad in 1933. It would be unfair, however, to accuse Gropius of naïve opportun-ism. His architectural vision was deeply socialistic in a way that antedated the Soviet system and looked beyond it. It was socialistic in a way that Igor Shafarevich could have appreciated the term, as expressed in his book *The Socialist Phenomenon*. It was socialistic in the same sense—perhaps almost lit-erally the same sense—as Johann von Leyden's Anabaptist commune in Muenster was. It bespoke the communality of wives and the communality of property in a concrete sense. Johann, it should be remembered, ordered

[4] Gropius, "Was erhoffen wir vom russischen Städtebau?" BMS Ger 208.2 (100), Collected Papers.

[5] Gropius, "Faith in Planning", BMS Ger 208 (149), Collected Papers.

[6] Ibid.

Figure 23. Bauhaus Dessau (in foreground)

the steeples of churches torn down, because no building was to be higher than any other in his egalitarian world. In the limited vocabulary of the architect, there are only a few terms available to express an attitude toward the transcendent, and the roof is one of the more important. The flat roof was an article of faith with the modern architect, no matter what the practical consequences (see Tom Wolfe's comments in *From Bauhaus to Our House* about the practicality of the flat roof along the fiftieth parallel). Whether it leaked or not was irrelevant. The flat roof was the main expression of the modern's anti-transcendental attitude.

But the connections between Bauhaus and the Soviets were more than merely theoretical. By the time Gropius gave his speeches in Leningrad, Ernst May, a member of the "Ring", the Berlin society of avant-garde architects during the 1920s (Mies van der Rohe was another member), was already in Moscow and functioning as organizer of the Soviet building commissariat and practical urban planning in the Soviet Union. Indeed, Gropius mentioned him explicitly in his speech. May was author of *The Socialistic City*. In addition, Gropius' hand-picked successor at Bauhaus-Dessau (fig. 23) was the avowed communist Hannes Meyer, who almost succeeded in politicizing the school out of existence. When the Nazis threatened to shut the school down in the early thirties, Gropius had to intervene and ask Mies van der Rohe to succeed Meyer, who at that point emigrated to the Soviet Union to practice architecture there. Because the State in the East Bloc countries was in absolute control of building, at least in the period following the Second World War, the box became for all intents and purposes the only type of building that was built, especially when it came to housing.

When I say "the box", I mean it quite literally. Each building is made up of little boxes for the most part six by eight meters in floor area. After the site was surveyed, a crane would begin piling box upon box until the building was finished. The whole process, according to Herr Dembrowsky, took six months, a time span I find astounding. Six *days* sounds like a lot of time to put together this type of building. But the six-month schedule may be the result of the type of workmanship involved. Everyone, it seems, who was involved in building also had another job on the side. Standard operating procedure was to steal half of what was intended for the job one was working on and sell it on the black market. The same was true of the collective farms. The farmers got a wage from the government to work the land and then stole half of what they produced and sold it on the black market. As a result, nothing much worked very well. Government subsidies covered the theft but eventually showed up as a huge foreign debt, forty-four billion dollars' worth.

When we arrive in Mrongoro, formerly Sensburg, late Saturday afternoon, the restaurants are closed, but the bars are still open. People are
lying dead drunk in the street or staggering around, looking in generally
bad shape. Herr Dembrowsky treats us to an ice cream cone, which has a
faintly chemical taste. I ask him if the drinking had always been this bad,
and he answers that it was worse before inflation set in, because vodka was
cheaper then. Every cloud has a silver lining, they say. Can skyrocketing
inflation be that bad if it cures Polish alcoholism? But then I hear the story
of the man and his daughter who drank some sort of fuel because it was
cheaper than vodka. "First they turned black like Negroes," said the
woman who told the story, "and then they died."

Chapter 7

SEMMERING, AUSTRIA

August 2, 1918

If it can be said of anyone, it can be said of Franz Werfel: the man led a charmed life. Unlike Walter Gropius, Werfel wasn't much of a soldier. Born in Prague of well-to-do Jewish parents in 1890, Werfel was interested in writing poetry when the war broke out, and the war, it must be admitted, did little to deter him from pursuing his interest. Assigned as a telephone operator in Galicia on the eastern front, Werfel had plenty of time to pursue his writing; in fact, he was working on a play most of the time he was there. At the end of June 1917, at the beginning of the Russian offensive, when Werfel was still at work on his play, he received an inquiry asking whether he would be interested in giving propaganda speeches in Switzerland. Shortly after this inquiry came from Vienna, the house where he had worked as telephone operator took a direct hit from a Russian artillery piece and was leveled to its foundation. Unlike Gropius, Werfel was nowhere to be seen when the house where he had been quartered was leveled by the enemy shell. He was already on a train heading west, looking forward to his job at the war press office.

The *Kriegspressequartier* had an impressive staff by anyone's reckoning. If an artillery shell had fallen there, as it had on Werfel's telephone office in Hodow, it would have wiped out most of modern German literature. Rainer Maria Rilke worked there, as did Stefan Zweig, Robert Musil, and Hugo von Hofmannstal. Another lesser light in the Teutonic literary firmament was Franz Blei, a friend of Werfel's from their days in Prague together. Another German-speaking Jew from Prague who shared their literary aspirations was Franz Kafka, who considered Werfel one of the great writers of the German language. Kafka wrote to his sister in 1913 that Werfel was a "miracle. When I read his book *The Worldfriend*, I thought I would go crazy with enthusiasm for it." [1] Werfel was flattered by Kafka's admiration, but he didn't reciprocate. He considered Kafka's work too obscure.

---

[1] Jungk, *Franz Werfel*, p. 44.

In November of 1917, Blei suggested that Werfel accompany him to the salon of a famous woman with cultural connections. Her name was Alma Mahler Gropius. Werfel immediately liked what he saw. The attractive thirty-eight-year-old woman—eleven years his senior—listened attentively in her hard-of-hearing way as the young poet spoke non-stop about his passion for Italian opera, the Russian Revolution, Christianity, and socialism. He stayed until late into the night.

Frau Mahler Gropius, for her part, seems to have been unimpressed. She referred to her first meeting with Werfel by describing him in her diary as that "fat, bow-legged Jew" with "thick lips", "watery, slanted eyes" (91), and tobacco-stained fingers. It may not sound like a case of love at first sight, but it was. An affair ensued. By December of 1917, Alma was pregnant, and she suspected that she was carrying Werfel's child. On the other hand, Walter Gropius, who checked into Vienna on his way back and forth to one front or the other (he had been most recently in Italy, training dogs to take messages through the trenches—an occupation that Alma found thoroughly repulsive), thought that the child was his, and of course Alma did nothing to disabuse him of this notion, even though she had at first tried to hide her pregnancy from him. Because Gropius was in such demand as a soldier, and Werfel was not, the younger man was left pretty much with an open field, a situation that he exploited to the full. So much so that gossip started making the rounds in the salons and cafés in Vienna. Everyone knew about the affair except the husband. Walter Gropius was the last to know.

By the summer of 1918, Werfel could plan on having a room of his own when he cared to stay at Haus Mahler in Semmering. Gropius, newly returned from the front with a fresh set of wounds, was living at the military hospital nearby. In late July, Werfel paid a visit to the seven-months-pregnant Alma. Frau Emmy Redlich also was there at the time, and in order to consummate their adultery, Alma and Franz had to engage in elaborate stratagems. Frau Redlich was first of all taken on a strenuous walk on the Kreuzberg and, following that, Alma played the entire second movement of Mahler's Eighth Symphony on the harmonium. Then, only two hours after everyone normally went to bed, Werfel could make his appearance in Alma's bedroom, where he quickly made up for lost time. "We made love", he wrote in his diary later. "I didn't spare her. Only with the coming of morning did I return to my own room" (99).

It was shortly after Franz Werfel had fallen asleep in his own bed that the maid woke him that morning to say that Alma was hemorrhaging. Werfel was beside himself with anxiety and guilt and was convinced that the bleeding was the result of his treatment of her that night. As he raced out of Haus Mahler and blindly off into the woods in an attempt to reach the local doctor, Werfel made a vow: If God would spare both mother and child, he would never look at another woman again. He would "remain true to Alma" for the rest of his life. "On the street" he promised he would not "lay his eyes on sexually arousing things" (100).

Considering that Werfel was promising to be true to a woman who was already married to another man, we can doubt that the Almighty was much impressed with his oath. But, as it turned out, the mother did not die, and the child was born safely—albeit two months prematurely. It was not the last time that Werfel was to make an oath, nor the last time that the Almighty seems to have granted his request. In 1940, while attempting to escape from the Nazis, who had overrun Austria and then France in short order, Werfel and Alma, now his wife, found themselves in Lourdes with no place else to go. Again Werfel made a vow. If God would permit them safe passage to America, he would write the story of Bernadette of Lourdes. Once again the Almighty seemed to grant him his wish. *Das Lied von Bernadette* went on to become a bestselling book and a motion picture hit. The U.S. Army bought fifty thousand copies of *The Song of Bernadette* to distribute to the troops.

Werfel is one of those figures who explode all categories of thought; he was a Jew who wrote about the Blessed Mother and gave lectures about the Catholic faith as the only basis for modern society but who never himself converted; a Jew who was married to an anti-Semite who had married two Jews. As a result of these anomalies, he has all but disappeared from the literary canon—in spite of the overwhelmingly favorable verdict of peers such as Franz Kafka, whose work is more appealing to modern sensibilities.

That summer morning in 1918, Alma Mahler was in serious trouble. On the same day that the bleeding started, she was rushed to Sanatorium Loew in Vienna, the clinic in which Gustav Mahler had died seven years before. Now it looked as if it was going to be Alma's turn to die. Werfel was kept apprised of the situation by telegram and telephone. On August 1, four days later, Werfel was told that Alma and the still-to-be-born child were both in the greatest danger. The doctors in attendance gave neither of them much of a chance to survive. Werfel, for his part, decided to fast as a way of persuading God to spare the lives of his child and its mother.

On the morning of August 2, 1918, Werfel called the hospital after a night of what he described as "paralysis-like sleep" that resembled being under hypnosis. Walter Gropius answered the phone and informed Werfel that during the night Alma had given birth to a baby boy. Both mother and child, he said, were doing relatively well. The news was enough to make Werfel feel that his prayers had been answered. "Inperdurable to me are you from this moment on, Lord of all Life", Werfel wrote in a letter to Alma, giving himself over to praising God. "And all of my being will not stop in giving you praise and blessing" (100).

Eight days after watching Alma being taken away to the hospital, Werfel finally got a chance to visit her there. He still was not completely sure that the child was his; however, just one look at the rapidly-breathing, weak, but sleeping baby in its crib convinced him. Not only did the baby resemble him, it bore an astonishing resemblance to his father, Rudolf Werfel. Years later Franz Werfel described this scene as the most important moment of his life. It was clearly the nexus of a number of powerful feelings: guilt, love, the sense of prayers answered, paternity, unworthiness, fear at being found out. One can imagine these feelings sweeping through the impressionable young poet all at once. Years later, in an allegorical work, Werfel described his feelings at the time:

> I was a Bohemian or something like that. I wrote poems and plays, and upon this cheap and ambitious activity I and the likes of me based the strange claim of exemption from the "civil order". . . . At the same time, however, I was convinced . . . that we too had offended not only against the civil order but against a higher world order.[2]

Werfel's confession was an archetypally unmodern moment. Full of remorse for sin, he admitted the existence of a higher order and his transgression against it, rather than rationalizing his sin and turning it into some sort of social movement.

Perhaps it was their guilty consciences that made Franz and Alma so sensitive to the appearance of the baby and—to them—the obvious resemblance to Werfel. When visitors came to the hospital room, both Alma and Werfel were distinctly ill at ease. One day both Gropius and Werfel were in the room together. Werfel was full of anxiety. "I trembled at the profundity of the situation", he wrote later,[3] but Gropius, still in the dark, doted on the sickly new-born infant, whom he thought was his own son.

[2] Monson, *Alma Mahler*, p. 193.
[3] Jungk, *Franz Werfel*, p. 102.

Chapter 8

WROCLAW, POLAND

April 20, 1990

Norbert Lemke's personal history epitomizes the trans-national character of Silesia. He grew up in a Polish-speaking family, but because of his father's unemployment he had to move to his grandmother's home near Gdansk toward the end of the 1930s. Both his grandmother and grandfather spoke nothing but German, so he quickly learned that language, just in time for the beginning of World War II, which he spent as a part of the Polish resistance against the Nazis. He was part of their equivalent of the Boy Scouts and spent his time involved in less dangerous jobs, such as carrying messages. Paul Frost, on the other hand, was born in Dzierzoniow, about forty miles south of Wroclaw. Then it was a German town known as Reichenbach. Herr Frost was older than Herr Lemke and so was inducted into the German *Wehrmacht* at the outbreak of the war. He spent his time in Estonia and remembers being quartered in a casino near Gdansk for a while, although, he says, he didn't win any money.

After the communists drove the Germans out of East Prussia, Stalin decided to replace them with Ukrainians, who for the most part had no experience with farms that were anywhere near the size and complexity of the German farms there. The intention on the part of the communists seems fairly clear. Keep the people isolated and deracinated and out of touch with each other so that they can't organize. Give them stolen goods so that they'll feel a little guilty about what they have. Send the Poles to the Urals; send the Germans to Murmansk; send the Ukrainians to *Ostpreussen*; put them all into concrete boxes; make them feel like aliens; deprive them of religion; make vodka cheap and readily available; and everyone will feel so alienated and disoriented, so cut off from any tradition that no one will make any trouble. And one more thing: destroy whatever you can find of the culture of the land you conquer, so that no one will have any sense that anything can be any different from what it is right now, which will be now and forever, communist world without end, amen. But this strategy did not work out according to plan, did it?

Figure 24. Apartments Wroclaw, Poland (in background)

Figure 25. Apartments Wroclaw, Poland

Figure 26. Apartments Kozanow, Poland

Human nature proved more resilient than the box makers imagined. Religion turned out to be something more than opium after all.

Forty-five years ago, Breslau had been turned into the fortress—*Festung Breslau*, it was called—that was to defend southeastern Germany from the advancing Soviet army. Hitler assigned a Ukrainian SS division to defend it, knowing that they would never surrender, because the Russians would never accept them as prisoners. So they fought to the last man and lost, and the Russian soldiers came into the town, which had been severely damaged by artillery fire already, and got roaring drunk and set the remaining houses on fire one by one, destroying what the artillery had missed. The job of restoring the town, Herr Lemke said, would have been much easier if it hadn't been set on fire, but boys will be boys, and Russian soldiers will be Russian soldiers, especially when they get their first chance to even up the score on German soil. But even after all the destruction, most of it unnecessary, the old buildings were still there. They were just lying slightly rearranged in the streets. Actually, they were still standing for the most part, even if gutted.

In a walk around the main square, Herr Lemke points out a building that is in the process of renovation, its façade still standing but its windows missing, and says that that is how most of the buildings looked after the war. So even the communists recognized that the center of town was too good to throw away. There is a mountain of rubble covered with grass not far from the center of town, and there are rows of the same ugly square apartment-boxes all over Wroclaw, but the tacit admission of a regime that could have started from zero was that they could not come up with anything better than the center of town and that the best thing they could do was restore it. I take it as a sign of hope and humility. All across former and current Germany one sees Bauhaus being torn down and the old architecture, the stuff that is traditionally German, being restored. It is as overt an admission as I have yet seen that, as far as architecture goes, we haven't come up with anything better in this century. Once that has been admitted, the only sensible option is to go back to the fork in the road where we made the wrong turn and start all over again.

Because Herr Lemke invited us to dinner at his house, I finally got to see the inside of one of the box apartments that dot the landscape of communist Poland like so many warts. Twenty years ago Herr Lemke and his wife and children lived in a larger apartment but one without any central heating. They had had to light and maintain a coal stove every day; and so they decided to move into their then-new apartment—all forty-eight square meters of it. This space—a little larger than eighteen feet by twenty-four feet, the size of a large American living room—is divided into a kitchen, a dining room, a bath, a living room, and a narrow bedroom a little wider than the bed itself. According to the determination of the communist state in Poland, each citizen has the right to seven to eleven square meters of apartment space. This "right" means that either that the state could have forced the Lemke family to live in an apartment almost half the size of the one they now had, which is to say one measuring seven by four meters (and there are apartments even smaller than that in this building), or that the current apartment was officially sufficient for seven people. Either way, it's not hard to understand why the Poles, the Hungarians, and the Czechs are not having large families. There is quite simply no place to put them. The apartment-box has had a devastating effect on the Polish family.

We sit down to a meal of *galumpki* at a table not much bigger than a card table in a dining room that allows room for a table and four chairs and little else. Over dinner Herr Lemke tells us that they now own the apartment and could pass it on to their grandchildren if they wished. In general, it takes a young couple twenty years to get an apartment of their own, so this is an appealing prospect to both generations. The question is whether the apartment buildings will last long enough to be passed on. Already there are visible signs of deterioration in the older buildings, those built twenty years ago or so. During the meal, Herr Lemke says that all of the apartments built after the war were built so shoddily that they will have to be torn down within the next ten years before they collapse onto the heads of the people living in them. The demise of so many ugly buildings is hardly bad news from an architectural point of view, but one wonders what is going to become of the inhabitants. Where are they going to live? One would have done better to rebuild the buildings that were destroyed during the war, but the rubble, which could have been reused, has long since been carted off to Russia or piled up in huge artificial grass-covered mountains around Wroclaw—the equivalent of the landfills around Chicago. I find myself wondering who is more adept at destroying cities, Americans or communists. We do it without the aid of war and saturation bombing. Is that a tribute to American efficiency?

Lemke says that when the apartments were owned by the state, they cost virtually pennies a month to rent. The heat for the apartments was created in furnaces miles away, which serviced a number of buildings. All the utilities are reckoned according to the size of the apartment, regardless of how much electricity or gas or heat actually is used. In response to my question as to whether the apartments are warm enough in winter, Herr Lemke says that except on the coldest nights he has to keep a window open all the time to cool the apartment off. All this was provided by the

Polish communist state for pennies a month—as long as the money held out, that is.

One thing to keep in mind is that Poland is now forty-four billion dollars in debt. One function of the borrowed money was to subsidize one or other of the necessities of life, as a way of keeping everyone more or less happy. That the more was inevitably less was not so much a function of the desire of the officials who created the system as of the human nature it was meant to contain. The ideal of the socialist state was control. Everything was structured with this in mind. So: vodka and apartments were cheap; a job was a right from which one could not be fired; and all systems of communication and interchange were built with a certain element of self-negation in mind, so that the frustration level of everyday life was never low enough to allow too much freedom of thought and initiative. The result was a system that approached total collapse the closer it got to total success.

Auxiliary Bishop Adam Dyczkowski of Wroclaw claims that the biggest family problem in Poland is the shortage of apartments in general and, by Western standards, the unbelievably small size of those that exist. Couples have small families because there is no room for big families, he says. They do not limit their families for selfish reasons as people do in the West. Horror stories abound. One man recently lost his job at a state-run business, which just went belly up because of the economic changes. He and his wife and child lived in a one-room apartment owned by the company he worked for. When he lost his job, he lost his apartment. As a result, the three of them had to move in with his grandmother, who also has a one-room apartment, but who has in addition three other people living with her! Hence seven people are now living in a one-room apartment. Under conditions like that, it's not surprising that families are small. There's hardly a chance for a couple to be intimate, much less beget children.

Chapter 9

SANATORIUM LOEW, VIENNA

August 25, 1918

On the morning of August 25, 1918, Walter Gropius arrived unexpectedly at the door of Alma's hospital room with an enormous bouquet of flowers in his hand. As he entered the room, he was struck by the intimate manner in which she was talking to someone on the telephone. A confrontation ensued, in which Gropius demanded an explanation; Alma at first demurred but then confessed to her affair with Werfel. Suddenly, to use the words Werfel used in his diary, Gropius "knew everything".[1] Now he was no longer in the dark about the paternity of the child and his wife's relations with Franz Werfel. Alma later wrote in her memoirs, "When I, incapable of lying, mentioned the name of Franz Werfel, Gropius fell to the floor as if struck by lightning" (183). The architect who had such an interest in *Klarheit* had been blind-sided by family relations once again. The locus of his betrayal was the dimly lit Haus Mahler, with its steeply pitched roof and small windows, its dark wood paneling, its candle-lit *Gemütlichkeit*, and the Kokoschka fresco over the fireplace. If, as Werfel claims, Gropius suddenly "knew everything", he probably knew where his wife had betrayed him. Haus Mahler with its dark corridors was proving to be an apt symbol of Gropius' increasingly labyrinthine, increasingly opaque domestic situation. Life with Alma was proving to be one unpleasant surprise after another.

The year 1918 was, from the German point of view, a year of collapse and unpleasant surprises as well. In addition to the collapse of the French town hall over his own head, Gropius lived through the collapse of his marriage and the collapse of the Austro-German military alliance as the Allied tanks finally broke through the German lines in the west. In each instance, no one suspected that things were going badly until the worst finally happened. In each instance, Gropius was more or less in the dark. "The majority of the population", writes Isaacs, his biographer, "was kept in the dark concerning the true military situation of Germany and the

---

[1] Jungk, *Franz Werfel*, p. 103.

Middle Powers" (184). Gropius' world collapsed in a particularly quick and dramatic fashion. After finding out the details of Alma's adultery at the end of August 1918, he was called back to the western front, only to be forced to retreat onto German soil. On September 29, Hindenburg and Ludendorff sued for peace; on October 26, Ludendorff was relieved of his position as commander-in-chief of the army; on October 29, mutiny broke out in Willemshaven among the sailors of the Imperial Navy; on November 9, the Weimar Republic was called into existence in Berlin, and one day later the Kaiser went into exile in Holland. On November 11, the armistice was signed. It led to the festering peace that led to World War II. It is difficult to think of a more devastating chain of events in the life of one man. "The collapse", Isaacs writes,

> meant personally the end of one segment of the life of Walter Gropius. He had served his country for more than four years and in the end had to live through the defeat of the fatherland and revolution at home. He returned from the field of battle a defeated man, both bodily and psychically wasted. The social order as he had known it, as it had been passed on to him, was destroyed, as were the traditions in which he had grown up. And in addition to all that, he lived with the tormenting certainty that he had lost his family (185).

Chapter 10

HARVARD UNIVERSITY

Commencement Day, June 1990

The 1990 Commencement at Harvard was being billed as an historic occasion, or at least a potentially historic occasion. Helmut Kohl, the chancellor of the German Federal Republic, which was soon to become just plain "Germany" once again, was to receive an honorary doctorate for having presided over the collapse of the Berlin Wall in November of 1989. He was at Harvard to receive an honorary doctorate because communism had collapsed on his watch and also, perhaps, because his son had graduated from Harvard the year before. Kohl's speech was being billed in advance as a latter-day equivalent of the Marshall Plan for Eastern Europe, its publicists playing on the fact that the original Marshall Plan also had been introduced at Harvard, forty-some years earlier.

The majority of the faculty could not have cared less. They had no dog in that fight, or, if they did, it was the wrong dog. A good number of them were sporting black, helium-filled balloons imprinted "Diversity", a code-word meaning that race and sex—or the ideologies that exploited them to their advantage—were to be the primary criteria for hiring faculty at Harvard. Given the mood of seemingly most of the faculty, the only thing that could have held their interest was the announcement that Kohl had ordered the re-annexation of the Sudetenland. Instead Kohl began his speech with a reference to his family.

"My son", said the chancellor of the German Federal Republic as he stepped up to the microphone at the podium across the lawn from Widener Library, "wanted me to relay a message to you. He told me to say that Mather House is the best house at Harvard."

The phrase crossed my mind again that night as I awoke in a cold sweat in one of the Mather House rooms—"cells" might be a better word. The clamminess was from the plastic-covered mattress; the cold, from the draft pouring into the open window just over the bed. The awakening was perhaps caused by the difference in temperature but more likely by the conversation going on in the quad beneath the window. Three undergraduates were sitting at the tables set up for the Class of 1940 (Pete Seeger was attending with his Asian wife, and Langdon Gilkey was there, too, wearing his love beads), and discussing the sexual exploits of one of the proctors at the halls. Mather House struck me then as a fitting place for this sort of conversation.

Perhaps, too, it was German patriotism that induced Kohl to mention Mather House. Walter Gropius didn't design it, but Walter Gropius is, in fact, the inventor of the modern undergraduate dormitory. It was invented at Bauhaus Dessau as a way of incorporating the Bauhaus way of life. According to Isaacs,

> The Studio Apartment House [*Das Atelierhaus*] . . . was a unique arrangement, because up to that time not one German university or Institute of Technology had a college dormitory [*Studentenwohnheim*] of its own; the fact that a number of students could live here under one roof contributed significantly to the feeling of togetherness that the Bauhausler experienced in Dessau. The Studio Apartment House was also the largest apartment building that Walter Gropius had actually completed up until that time (358).

The Bauhaus vision of communal living found its most complete expression in university architecture in a university setting—a fact that remains true if unappreciated today. The particular form of libertine socialism that Bauhaus propagated found its most congenial setting in the universities of the West. Living in a college dormitory has become, willy-nilly, an introduction to Bauhaus values. College education has become the equivalent of a four-year course in socialism. Living in Mather House was like four years of free love in the Death Star.

Mather House was designed by the firm of Shepley, Bulfinch, Richardson, & Abbott of Boston. It was named after Increase Mather, the Puritan divine, but it looks like the inspiration for the Star Wars movie set. This combination of Bauhaus and Puritanism—both of which see ornament as sinful—has a certain consistency, I suppose. It could be said that the modern age is the fulfillment of the forces set in motion by the Reformation. But the impression one gets is more of incongruity than anything else. It is an incongruity typical of any institution whose god is the *Zeitgeist*. What would the Puritan divines have thought about the sexual license of Weimar Germany institutionalized in Harvard architecture? It's hard to say. But then too, what would they have thought of the sexual license unleashed in Germany as a result of the Renaissance? Again, it's hard to say.

Mather House is a combined low- and high-rise structure, joined by an enclosed quadrangle. It is made out of poured concrete and has all the warmth and *Gemütlichkeit* that concrete radiates. In order to enter the rooms in the low rise, one climbs free-standing, poured-concrete stairs—

the largest in the world—from which one steps off onto a concrete platform, then through a locked door into a long, curved, and windowless
corridor whose walls are also of the same poured concrete. Now the Star
Wars ambiance really becomes apparent. At regular intervals along the corridor, there are large black panels, which, upon closer inspection, turn out
to be doors, doors that lead nowhere. They are held in place by electro-
magnets and, with the press of a button, will swing open into the hallway,
blocking off one segment of it. The architect who designed Mather House
went to Harvard, but has become so annoyed at the response to his building that he will no longer answer questions about it. So the mysterious
black doors are popularly explained in two ways; they provide fire control
or they are there for riot control. The latter explanation is advanced by the
architecture student who says that the architect of Mather House is not
answering questions.

Of the two explanations, the one about riot control is the more plausi-
ble. Poured concrete, the main component of the building, is not a particularly combustible substance. Other older buildings made out of wood and
other materials that burn readily lack the doors. And there is the evidence
of the times. The building was built in 1970, at the high point of campus
disturbances. It was at the end of the spring semester of 1970 that Richard
Nixon ordered the invasion of Cambodia, which had as its immediate effect a number of riots on campuses across the country, most notably at
Kent State (Ohio), where a number of students were killed by National
Guard troops. In 1970, some graduation ceremonies didn't take place, as a
way of forestalling more disruption. In the spring of 1970, many students
received their diplomas by mail. And, as Gropius himself once said (in a
speech titled "Architektur an der Harvard Universität"), "Good architecture must reflect the life of the times." [1] Or as he said in "Twentieth Century Collegiate Architecture", the speech in which he tried to drum up
support for his own Harkness Commons complex, the first modern building at Harvard: "Architecture is said to be a true mirror of the life and social behavior of a period. If that is true, we should be able to read from its
present features the driving forces of our times." [2]

The signs of the times are nowhere more legible than in the architecture of Mather House. Mather House reflects the shift at a place like Harvard in particular and the universities in the United States in general away

[1] Gropius, "Architektur an der Harvard Universität", in Hartmut Porbst and Christian
Schädlich, *Walter Gropius*, vol. 3, *Ausgewählte Schriften* (Berlin: Verlag für Architektur und technis-
che Wissenschaften, 1988), p. 166.
[2] Gropius, "Twentieth Century Collegiate Architecture", BMS Ger 208 (110), Collected
Papers.

from the education of gentlemen and toward crowd control. Mather House is as good an example as any of the paradoxical results of the mechanization of the intellectual life, which has characterized the modern age. In the name of the rationalization of life (remember *Wohnmaschinen?* remember Le Corbusier's dictum: "A house is a machine for living in"?), morality and religion were scrapped as internal controls on behavior. Colleges were no longer to function *in loco parentis*. As a result the university had to build buildings to withstand the uncontrolled passions of its undergraduate population, buildings that would not be damaged by students who were unable or unwilling to control their impulses. As a result, Harvard got into architectural crowd control and into building structures that looked a lot like—well, prisons.

It is the paradox of modern education in stone; the more the educators idealize their students as Rousseauan innocents, the more the architects have to come up with prisons to contain the violence these theories unleash. In this sense, Mather House is not all that much different from the Projects on the South Side of Chicago, or the elementary schools without windows that sprang up as the architectural response to the open-classroom theories of the sixties.

The rationalization of social interaction through the abrogation of moral law and religion led to the more or less complete breakdown of social behavior, which necessitated an architecture of control. By giving themselves over to the so-called scientific world view, the inhabitants of the *Wohnmaschinen* soon found that they were being housed like rats in some huge laboratory experiment that had long since run out of control; and before long they started acting accordingly. If urban planning were explained in terms of nuclear energy, then what goes on in the South Side Projects and the average college dormitory can fairly be described only as social meltdown. "We live in a period of reshuffling our entire life", Gropius wrote in 1940. "The old society went to pieces under the impact of the machine; the new one is still in the making." [3]

Gropius put himself in the paradoxical position of wanting to fight fire with fire. He built "apartment machines" as a way of freeing people from the mechanization of modern life, or at least that is how the explanation goes. However, in reality, the machine was attractive for other reasons. It was neat and clean and bespoke clarity in a way that the past, with its tangle of history and ornamentation and conflicting human relations, did not. The *Wohnmaschine* was to provide intellectual *Klarheit* by organizing family

[3] Gropius, "Statement on the Nature of Modern Architecture", BMS Ger 208 (40), Collected Papers.

life according to the principles of modern industry. It bespoke the geometrization of sexual life, so to speak, and through its implementation in architecture, human relations were to take on similarly transparent, similarly orderly modalities. "Our houses are museums, instead of places to live in", Gropius writes in "Ornament and Modern Architecture" (1938), referring to the sort of house he wants to replace.

> The blight of ornamentation has fallen on all our intimate surroundings. The human being, lost in the increasing chaos of mechanization, became timid and uncertain how to give expression to his inward intentions; and imagination became stunted. The *horror vacui* broke loose, filling any decent empty space on walls, floors, furniture and lampshades with inorganic emblems, symbols, ornaments as supposed sedatives for the troubled soul. A revolution was due.
>
> Modern architecture represents the vital reaction to this chaotic confusion—a vigorous attempt to rid us of these hopeless narcotics and to find again a true expression which may mirror our very life of the machine age.[4]

In order to get to your sleeping quarters in Mather House, you first enter the common room off the corridor with its riot-control doors. This room is small and notable for its lack of depth; it is one wide horizontal rectangle facing a large plate-glass window, giving it all the coziness of a display window in Macy's. Then one makes a turn and goes down a flight of stairs into a dimly lit foyer, which leads onto the four bedrooms and the shared bath. Actually, "shared bath" takes on a new meaning in Mather House. Each individual bathroom is separated from its neighbor on either side by a pair of fire doors, so that if all the fire doors were opened at once, all the bathrooms would be merged into one long bath-corridor that would go the entire length of the building. As a result of this preprogrammed assault on privacy, people tend to wander in and out of the bathrooms at will. As I am ready to step into the shower, a young Asian lady walks into the bathroom and begins to wash out her Styrofoam cooler in the sink.

The scenario at Mather House is something like that schlocky sixties potboiler *The Harrad Experiment* ("the sex manifesto of the free-love generation"), acted out in the basement of the Death Star. It is *Weimar Republik* values acted out in a Bauhaus setting. In the East, socialism took over whole countries; in the West, it took over only certain institutions—academe being the most prominent. Practically every adolescent who goes away to college, to live in a high-rise, co-ed dorm somewhere or other will certainly be exposed to its rigors. The communality of wives and the

---

[4] Gropius, "Ornament and Modern Architecture", BMS Ger 208 (23), Collected Papers.

communality of property espoused by Johann von Leyden in Muenster are nowhere so well implemented as on the campuses of the universities of the West, where those who don't want to end up working at McDonald's or in the army are subjected to a four-year intensive course of free love in the Death Star.

Bauhaus is the physical embodiment of this form of living. Or as Gropius himself said ("Twentieth Century Collegiate Architecture"):

> What we need is a new code of visual values. So long as we flounder about in a limitless welter of borrowed artistic expression, we shall not succeed in giving form and substance to our own culture, for this implies selective choice and limitation to those artistic means which best express the ideas and spiritual directions of our time. . . . The impact of the environment on a young man during his college studies is certainly decisive. If the college is to be the cultural breeding ground for the coming generation, its attitude should be creative, not imitative.
>
> Therefore, the student needs the real thing, not buildings in disguise. So long as we do not ask him to go about disguised in mediaeval garb, it seems absurd to build a brand-new college gymnasium in pseudo-Gothic style in order to "conform" with some of the existing pseudo-Gothic college buildings surrounding it. For how can we expect our youngsters to become bold and fearless in thought and action if we encase them timidly in sentimental shrines feigning a culture which has long since disappeared? . . . The physical and spiritual functions determining the design of a building are interdependent. It is an anachronism to express the physical functions with the newest technical means, but the spiritual ones by borrowing a historical shell from the past.[5]

"A true modern architect", Gropius writes in "Ornament and Architecture", is one "who tries to shape our new conception of life".[6] He is one "who refuses to live by repeating the forms and ornaments of our ancestors".[7] "Our confused mind will become proud and confident at last in having at our disposal such brilliant means for shaping the image of our modern life." [8] Gropius, who is now writing in English, having arrived at Harvard after a stay of four years in England, then makes use of a curious locution to describe the architectural tradition he wants to revolutionize. He calls it "our *bastard civilization* of borrowed ornaments" (my emphasis).[9]

---

[5] Gropius, "Twentieth Century Collegiate Architecture".
[6] Gropius, "Ornament and Modern Architecture".
[7] Ibid.
[8] Ibid.
[9] Ibid.

The choice of words is interesting. Probst and Schädlich in their book on Gropius' architecture translate the phrase "bastard civilization" into German as "*verfälschte Zivilisation*" ("counterfeit civilization"). They could have used the word "bastard", which is also a word in German, but apparently chose not to, either because the term was not normally used in that fashion (then again, it isn't normally used that way in English either) or because of the term's discomforting psychological implications. In the latter case, the implications are clear; the "new code of visual values", which is modern architecture, is an attempt to "overcome our bastard civilization of borrowed ornaments".

Twenty years before Gropius gave this speech at Harvard, the notion of a "bastard civilization" had more than figurative meaning in his life. Gropius' wife had just given birth to Franz Werfel's son, a bastard who was to die in a matter of months. Gropius' domestic life was proving to be the antithesis of *Klarheit*. Haus Mahler, with its *gemütlich* wood paneling and dark passages, was the locus of his betrayal—not that Gropius had any special claim on marital fidelity, however. He had betrayed Gustav Mahler, and Frau Mahler had betrayed him in Haus Mahler in turn. Then within a matter of weeks of the birth of Martin Johannes Werfel, Germany lost the war, and the Kaiser went into exile. It was out of this concatenation of events that the ideology of modern architecture was born. Industrial forms were to be superimposed over domestic arrangements—partly as a way of creating *Klarheit*, partly out of simple revenge on an institution that had betrayed him after he had betrayed it, but especially as a rationalization of the sexual license that had preceded the unhappy birth and most definitely followed it, as well.

"Under the impression of these experiences", writes Isaacs referring to the collapse of the German–Austrian powers after the war,

> [Gropius'] attitude toward politics and society, toward work and life underwent a radical change. Suddenly he was overcome—"as if hit by a beam of light", he was to say later—the recognition dawned on him that he had to convert and adjust himself to new times and new relationships. The former conservative became almost overnight a progressive. It was a sudden inner transformation, which he described in his memoirs with the following expressive phrase: "After the war it dawned on me . . . that the old crap was finished." And then as if trying to make up in weeks what he had missed in years, he threw himself back into his work—most urgently in the reopening of his architecture office and bringing his personal life in order (188).

Figure 27. Walter Gropius, 1920

Chapter 11

VIENNA, AUSTRIA

November 1918

Walter Gropius was demobilized on November 18, 1918—just in time for
the revolution then sweeping both Austria and Germany. On the evening
of Easter Monday, April 16, 1917, Vladimir Ilyich Lenin arrived to a
hero's welcome at the red-banner-festooned Finland Station in Petrograd.
"The predatory imperialist war is the beginning of a civil war all over Europe", he said to the cheering crowd. "Any day now you shall see the collapse of European imperialism." Lenin, it is clear, saw the events in Russia
as the prelude to a trans-European revolution that would lead to a world
revolution. On November 12, 1918, one day after Emperor Charles I left
Vienna for exile in Switzerland, the revolution came to Austria. Franz
Werfel, who was almost court-martialed during the war for giving incen-
diary speeches while in the employ of the imperial propaganda ministry,
joined the "Red Guard", a revolutionary cell founded by a number of literary men of his acquaintance. On the morning of the twelfth, Werfel
showed up at Alma's apartment to ask for her blessing. Then he was off to
a huge demonstration on the Ringstrasse in front of the Parliament building, where the flag-waving of the Red Guard and their subsequent
attempt to force an entrance into the parliament building led the soldiers
present to fire upon the crowd, killing two and wounding a number of
others. Werfel escaped without injury. On the evening of the twelfth,
when he returned to Alma's apartment exhausted, she disgustedly kicked
him out and turned her affections to Gropius, who spent the next few
days running around after Werfel, trying to keep him from falling into the
hands of the police. Werfel's revolutionary ardor soon cooled, and he
found his way back to the coffee houses and literary life he had left at the
beginning of the war. But Gropius, who lacked both Werfel's naïveté and
his ardor, was ready to embark upon a revolution of a much more calcu-
lating and, as a result, more long-lasting variety.

By the end of 1918, Gropius had left Vienna, in order (in Alma's
words) to "build a new life for us" in Germany. He had reopened his architectural office in Berlin and had made contact with the artistic avant-

garde there. Around Christmas of that year, he was working on an architectural manifesto with Bruno Taut, which declared that "architecture was
the foremost bearer of spiritual powers and molder of our sensibility"
(195). This same architecture was to bring about "a complete revolution
in the cultural sphere" (195). Around the same time, he wrote to his
mother: "I've been transformed from Saul to Paul through all the interior
suffering I've experienced during the war. Now my only wish is to be
united after a long period in the desert with people of like mind and then
to get happily down to work" (196).

    There were certainly enough like-minded people in Berlin as a result of
the lost war. Mies van der Rohe, among others, had founded the "radical"
and "revolutionary" group of artists that came to be known as the November Group. One of Gropius' first architectural projects of this period
was the *Wohnberg*, the "apartment mountain", a utopian project that was
never built. The *Wohnberg* was to be a huge, thirty-story apartment building in triangular form, an upturned rowboat in appearance. Gropius envi-
sioned four kinds of apartments for the *Wohnberg*: one for people living
alone, one for "couples bound together in a love or work relationship"
(199), one for families with children, and one for old people. According to
the notes he wrote to accompany the *Wohnberg* design, Gropius foresaw a
change in social structures. The *Wohnberg* was to precede and facilitate this
change by making the fundamental social unit not the family or the community but rather the individual, upon whom a whole new social order
would arise. In Gropius' utopia, there would be no more family responsibility; the woman was to be emancipated from household work by the
creation of common kitchens, cafeterias and laundries, leading to a complete equality between the sexes.

    In April of 1919, Gropius began his tenure as director of the Bauhaus
in Weimar. In the first Bauhaus Manifesto, issued in 1919, Gropius called
for the construction of the "Cathedral of the future" (200): "Architecture
and sculpture and painting, rising up out of the hands of millions of
craftsmen as the crystal symbol of this new Religion" (210). Gropius was
very clear in this regard. He was not in the business, he wrote to his
mother, of designing "correct" lamps, but rather "to take part in a new
community which is going to create the new Man in a new environment" (211). Bauhaus wasn't just a new style of architecture; it embodied a new way of living in conscious revolution against traditional values.
The new architecture was simply the quickest and most effective way to
concretize this new way of life in the world. Gropius saw Bauhaus Weimar as

the beginning of the European cultural revolution, which has to come. The confrontation between the old world view, which is based on classical learning, and a completely new way, which is Gothic and finds its symbols in expressionism. It's no coincidence that this struggle is breaking out here in Weimar, the bulwark of the classical tradition. My powers are beginning to grow in this struggle. I am going to proceed hard and without compromise, even if it takes its toll on my nerves (235).

In a speech he gave, entitled "Architecture in an Independent People's State", Gropius proposed his own version of revolution, a cultural revolution, which succeeded in both East and West, and which seems to have outlived the more politically-oriented revolution in the East:

> The thrones have been cast down, but the old spirit still has its hold on the entire country with its tenacious roots. What this country needs is a new communal spirituality suitable for all the people. . . . We're still deeply enmired in the old sins. Not a political but only a cultural revolution can liberate us completely (288).

"Deeply enmired in the old sins" ("*Wir stecken Tief im Sumpf der alten Sünden*") is an interesting formulation also of Gropius' domestic situation in 1919. Gropius had left Vienna in late 1918 "to start a new life" in Germany, according to Alma Mahler's formulation. That Gropius wanted to do what he wanted to do and Alma wanted to do likewise, and that there was no one place where both could do what they wanted seems closer to the truth. Gropius wanted to found Bauhaus, but Alma was too closely tied to Viennese cultural and social life and had, according to Isaacs, little interest in Bauhaus or the people involved in it, with the exception of Paul and Lily Klee. Alma was also deeply involved in promoting Mahler's music, and Gropius seems to have had no interest in that either. In addition, Alma seems to have had no intention of giving up Franz Werfel as her lover. In an entry dated December 15, 1918 (in other words, shortly after Gropius left for Berlin), Alma notes that she spent a "glorious night with Werfel" (189). Gropius in his correspondence with Alma shows increasing annoyance that she refuses to send Werfel on his way. "I have the feeling that I'm nothing to you at all, and that you don't miss me. . . . Above all I'm waiting for you to get rid of Werfel. . . . But nothing has happened. It's all empty words. You don't have the guts to do it and instead do nothing but play games with me, unfinished games, that are going to take their revenge on both of us" (190).

Alma, for her part, hardly seems to have had a faithful bone in her body, but she reacted negatively to her husband's suggestion that they divorce. At one point she suggested that a suitable arrangement might be that she spend half a year with Gropius and the other half with Werfel, an arrangement that Gropius rejected out of hand: "Do me a favor, my dear", he wrote back, "and don't offer me halves" (226).

Gropius, on the other hand, wanted to force the issue. "We have to achieve some clarity [*Klarheit*] here", he said, using a favorite expression (226). "The sickness of our marriage requires an operation." And then later, switching from the imagery of divorce to annulment, he adds, "Our marriage was never really a marriage" (226).

When Gropius talked about being "enmired in the old sins", however, he was probably referring to more than his wife's behavior. In the fall of 1919, more than one year before his divorce from Alma was granted, Gropius began an affair with Lily Hildebrandt, a thirty-one-year-old married woman from Stuttgart. According to Isaacs, what brought the two of them together was "a common interest in Art as well as a life which sought new modes of expression and liberation from the shackles of convention" (229). The love affair lasted four years, the four years that corresponded with the beginning of Bauhaus in Weimar. During the duration of their affair, Gropius wrote Hildebrandt letters in which he reminisced about clandestine meetings with her in hotel rooms. "When you get hot with thoughts of me", he wrote at one point, "put a flower between your magnificent thighs and then send it to me by mail" (230). Or at another, "I want to bore through you with the sword of my love" (235). At the same time, he formulated a quasi-poetic theory of human relations, which, coincidentally (or perhaps not so coincidentally), fit in with the parameters of his own complicated sexual life at the time. "I have to get used to traveling like a shooting star through the heavens", he writes to Lily, "and am just beginning to live hand to mouth and full of adventure, casting my anchor nowhere and breaking off where something is about to begin. This is obviously my fate. I am now a sacrificial lamb, and watch as my blood is shed . . ." (249).

So Gropius falls upon the thorns of life; he bleeds. And his architecture is based upon a sociology of human relations which in turn rests on the exigencies of keeping a number of affairs going at once. This is the human matrix out of which the *Wohnmaschine* grows (the speech of this name was written in 1919): the machine for living is a mechanical surrogate for the home. It is designed to facilitate mechanical sex between interchangeable partners as opposed to monogamous marriage. It appears in specifically mechanical shapes that embody the Bauhaus philosophy, which is to break down the old ideas of exclusivity in marriage, privacy, and the irreplaceable and unique characteristics of the person, specifically the spouse. In their place one finds the rhetoric of industrialism, the mechanization of

Figure 28. Lily Hildebrandt (on ladder)

sexual life, interchangeable parts and partners, and a complete repudiation of the notion of the home as a private place and a refuge from the world and its instrumental values.

The beginning of Gropius' tenure as director of Bauhaus Weimar corresponds with his divorce from Alma, his involvement in numerous affairs with different women, and his subsequent rationalization of his own complicated sexual life in letters to each of them. Out of this personal matrix came the merging of industrial and domestic styles of architecture (they had remained separate before the war) into one ideologically oriented architecture, which had as its *raison d'être* the revolutionizing of human, specifically domestic, relations.

Before the war, Gropius had built modern factories and houses in the vernacular style. After the war, he built houses that looked like modern

Figure 29. Die Weissenhofsiedlung, Stuttgart, 1927

factories—all of the great socialist worker housing projects (the Weissen-hofsiedlung in Stuttgart, for example) took place in the twenties under the sponsorship of the Social Democrats in Germany—which were to bring about the supposed "rationalization" of human relations.

In a speech given in 1940, Gropius talked about the "idea of rationaliza-tion" as "the outstanding characteristic of the new architecture".[1] The statement was much truer than he knew. The new architecture was in ef-fect his rationalization of the life of sexual liberation he was leading at the time. Bauhaus wasn't so much a style of design as a style of life that could best be fostered by the incorporation of industrial design into personal life. Those big machines representing impersonal laws of nature were to give one the impression that sexual behavior wasn't so important after all. It was easier to conduct an affair in a sleeping car on the Orient Express than in a bedroom full of knick-knacks and pictures of the husband and children.

In the official description of the Weissenhof apartment complex in Stuttgart, a collaboration of Gropius, Mies van der Rohe, and Le Corbus-ier among others, one hears the deeper meaning quite clearly: "The prob-

[1] Gropius, "Statement on the Nature of Modern Architecture".

lem of the new apartment is basically a spiritual problem, and the struggle for the new apartment is one aspect of the larger struggle for new life-styles" (*neue Lebensformen*)" (387). The new architecture was simply a con-crete way of implementing the lives that Gropius and Mies van der Rohe were living at the time. It was rationalization in the deepest sense of the word.

What that life was like can be garnered from the letters Gropius wrote at the time. In 1919, right around the time of his affair with Lily Hilde-brandt and the divorce from Alma, he wrote to the latter, announcing, "I have burned my ships recklessly behind me and have decidedly drawn the conclusions of the new era and dedicated myself to them both internally and externally. . . . I am fighting against a world full of Philistines, but be-hind me stand legions" (239). At around the same time, he wrote a letter to Lily Hildebrandt, describing among other things his social relations at Bauhaus. "No, my heart, I am not in love with any other woman; I haven't kissed any, either, not even at the most recent [Bauhaus] party. However, I have noticed that I've reached an age and a spiritual condition [*Geistesverfassung*] that women find attractive, because many of them are making passes at me. You shouldn't get upset, though. After our sweet sat-iation in Frankfurt, I'm in an erotic-free period and am completely caught up in my work" (232). As his biographer says, the claim that Gropius was attractive to women was "hardly braggadocio" on his part. Bauhaus pro-vided the raw materials for and the rationale behind the sexual "liberation" of Walter Gropius. By the second semester of his first year there, he was also sexually involved with a young, attractive student–widow (as a result of the war and the mortality rate among German soldiers, there were lots of these around) by the name of Maria Beneman, to whom he was also writing rhapsodic love letters, or, perhaps more accurately, love letters in the Bauhaus style. In a deflating aside, Isaacs says that the letters to Mrs. Beneman and Mrs. Hildebrandt were remarkably similar in tone. They all sound like the Gestalt Prayer of Fritz Perls.

"MARIA", Gropius begins in all capitals,

> I am a shooting star in this universe, I know neither anchor nor chain, I re-tire to the bushes when I suffer and appear among others only when I am full and giving. I bind myself nowhere and to no one. I lighten things up wherever I go and create life that way. I am a thorn and as a result a strong and dangerous tool!!! I love without restraint, the high and eternal intensity.
>
> You wanted me and I gave myself to you, and it was beautiful and pure, two stars united their conflagration; however:
>
> Don't threaten me!
>
> Don't demand anything of me!

Don't expect anything from me!

Because everything that human beings give to each other is gift. I know
nothing, I promise nothing, I drink in your warmth gratefully and one day
the sword will rise out of me again. Right now though I'm sitting in a
thousand torments in the ashes. I am without peace and innerly torn and
need peace and solitude (244).

After that panegyric to love in the Bauhaus manner, Gropius adds that
Frau Beneman should behave herself when the two of them appear in
public, especially at the Bauhaus soirées: "I would prefer that people not
know about my intimate relations because that's my own completely private business. That's why I appear indifferent to you in public. Please understand, and don't think that it's anything personal" (244).

Given his personal life at the time, it is understandable that certain characteristics would appeal to Gropius in the social realm. Because he was en-
tangled with so many women at the time, he would have a penchant for
clear geometrical forms as compensation. Lightness would also be attractive; his architecture would be the clear geometric light of reason applied
to human relations. A man in his position would like to be able to claim
that he had nothing to hide, and so lots of plate-glass would be an attractive form of compensation. The new man would not be bound to any one
place, any one home, any one country, or any one woman. He would
know "neither anchor nor chain". In a letter to Lily Hildebrandt around
the same time, he wrote, "I wish I had you in my arms again to drink in
Lethe and forgetfulness, to shed all earthly heaviness, to float, to fly, to
breathe in the sun, [but] I sit deep below in shadows. . . . Perhaps I am a
very difficult person, difficult to understand, unwilling to make conces-
sions, but then again also completely without false sentimentality too"
(245).

The description sounds remarkably like the façade of a Bauhaus building. The element of rationalization is evident in both. Free love is lifted on
the wings of the ever-powerful technology of reinforced concrete, and the
birth-control device is to free man from his bondage to flesh, soil, and tradition. Instead of living close to the ground, married to one woman in the
welter of family responsibility and conflict, the brave new world proposed
by the Bauhausler will consist of individuals living above the fray—twelve
stories above it, to be precise, in cubicles all by themselves behind plate-
glass windows with nothing to hide. This relationship ostensibly combines
the best of both worlds; man will be henceforth simultaneously angel and
beast. Instead of the *politikon zoon*, sustained and defined by a plenitude of
human relationships, the most basic of which is the family, which connects
him to the soil and the past, the new man will live without binding and

Figure 30. Cartoon of Thomas Theo Heine, "The Struggle against Ornamentation"

inhibiting connections in a habitat finally suitable to his newly achieved status as "free spirit", the word Gropius used to describe himself after his divorce came through. He will "float" and "fly" and "breathe in the sun" through plate-glass windows twelve stories in the air. The new architecture will give man the sense that he is above it all, that he is not bound to one place or woman.

In Gropius' relations with his lady friends there is no artifice, no ornament, no façade of "false sentimentality". Bauhaus is free love according to the new order. It is human relations stripped down to essentials, as a materialist scientist of that age would describe them. The things that used to be hidden behind ornament and molding—the plumbing, for example—are now to be exposed in all of their utilitarian glory. Now the plumbing itself is the ornament. There would be no "false sentimentality". The pipes would become the message. Reason and openness become the ultimate rationalizations, the ultimate anesthetic for a troubled conscience. The attack on the privacy of the home was simply another way for the Bauhausler to say that he had "nothing to hide". And he made that claim at the urging of his troubled conscience, just as Gropius does in his letters to his lady friends.

Having three or four women on the line at one time probably leads one to think favorably about industrial techniques of mass production as well. The adulterer in this circumstance is a mechanical reproduction of the husband. Gropius said more than once that his idea of the new home came from the image of Ford automobiles following each other off the assembly line. The image of the home as a unique place bound to a particular piece of earth and unique persons was built on the institution of matrimony and monogamy in which one man bound himself to one woman in sexual fidelity until death. The unique and irreplaceable value of the persons involved was exalted and maintained by the exclusivity of the union. In fact, the monogamous and faithful union until death is the only sexual expression worthy of the uniqueness of the human persons who make it up. If the union is not permanent, then the people are in a certain sense replaceable, and once that step has been made the techniques of the industrial revolution as applied to human relations begin to make more and more sense.

The home, then, in the traditional view, is the embodiment of the uniqueness and irreplaceability of those bound together in the marital relationship. A particular man is bound to a particular woman and bound to a particular piece of soil in a particular city and country, and the children arising from that union will inherit the characteristics of both as well as the traditions—the household gods, in an older sense—peculiar to that family. The desire to build houses that looked like factories bespoke a deeper desire to restructure and materialize the family. It bespoke a desire to remake the world over in the image of the lives that the architect and his followers were living. Gropius was right, the new architecture bespoke "rationalization" in just about every sense of the word.

Chapter 12

HARVARD UNIVERSITY

June 1990

Peabody Terrace is the high-rise apartment house for married students at Harvard University. It was built in 1963–64 by Sert, Jackson, Gourley. Jose Luis Sert was Gropius' hand-picked successor to lead the architecture department. Peabody Terrace is Bauhaus "worker housing" in the late classic style. In the sixties, Cambridge, Massachusetts, finally got the kind of high-rise building Gropius had been proposing as the "direct embodiment of the needs of our age" since his days in Berlin in 1919.

Michael Waldstein, a native of Salzburg, Austria, lived for three years in Peabody Terrace while studying theology at Harvard in the eighties. Waldstein lived there with his wife and four children, in a two-bedroom apartment on the seventh floor. In addition to living in Austria and Cambridge, the Waldsteins have also lived in Italy and California, and they currently own a home in the suburbs outside of South Bend, Indiana, where he teaches theology at the University of Notre Dame. Waldstein thinks that Peabody Terrace is "smartly built". The space inside the apartment is "used economically; the proportions are good; there are no dead corners." But his ultimate verdict is that the building is "not humane". "The atmosphere is dreary. It gets to you after a while. You feel sort of hollow." As a result, Waldstein was happy to move into a house with a yard. Peabody Terrace was more "a storage box than a home for three years".

On the plus side of things, the apartment was well built and designed. It also had cross ventilation so that it was cool on the warmest evenings; however, living on the seventh floor gave the Waldsteins the feeling that they were not really part of a household. "You always had the sense that you were hovering or flying or in storage and not in a particular place. It's not a good thing to be that high up all the time". According to Waldstein, the building lacked *Bodenständigkeit*, a German word which can be translated simultaneously as "stability" and "connection to the soil".

"Living with a yard on the ground in a house among other houses", he continued, "gives one the sense of being more in control and more at peace." Being up in the air all the time, on the other hand, gives one a sense of "being hollowed out, as if you hadn't eaten for a while".

The close proximity of so many people had a paradoxical effect on sociability. "One would think that buildings like that would be a beehive where everyone gets to know everyone else, but the exact opposite was true", Waldstein continued. Instead people had to develop a certain insensitivity to each other as their only way of maintaining privacy. "The building gives you the sense that you have to shield the little space, the little privacy you have from others. Other people become intruders, and as a result people put on this tough skin to protect themselves. You need more space to be sociable. The people who live in houses on the ground", he says, referring to where he lives now, "tend to be much more neighborly because there is less of a threat".

During his three years' living in Peabody Terrace, Waldstein noticed that the only married people who maintained contact with each other in the building were those who had children. The explanation may be that taking care of children in a high-rise building is a ritual that involves the mothers' going to the playground or the ground floor playroom at regular times, thereby providing themselves with the opportunity to socialize. Those who were married but had no children, on the other hand, had little or no reason to come in contact with anyone else. Or it may be that having children is such an unusual act at Harvard that those who do it feel part of some special fraternity. Either way, children were the one thing that broke down the isolation. "We observed people without children who lived there for years and didn't talk to anyone."

Waldstein claims that living in a place like Peabody Terrace is possible but that he would "prefer not to". The thing he noticed the most after moving into his new house in South Bend is its *Bodenständigkeit*. "It's a place of my own; a place where I can rest. That sense of being at home, of being at rest is something I never got in three years at Peabody Terrace, and now I have it after two months of living in this house."

Gropius campaigned his entire life for ten- to twelve-story workers' housing, initially against the Prussian zoning ordinance limiting it to three or four stories to keep down population density. In Peabody Terrace as in the Projects on the South Side of Chicago, as in the poured-concrete apartments of Nowa Huta, he got what he wanted. By the end of his life he had the dangerous satisfaction of being able to see people all over the world living as he wanted them to live, as he himself wanted to live as expressed in his letter to Lily Hildebrandt: "to shed all earthly heaviness, to float, to fly, to breathe in the sun".

Jose Luis Sert was dean in the school of design from 1953 to 1969. His firm also built the Carpenter Center for the Visual Arts (fig. 32) in collaboration with Le Corbusier in 1961–62. The Carpenter Center is generally described by those at Harvard as two grand pianos copulating. The entrance looks like an off-ramp of the Verrazano Narrows Bridge. In order for the ramp to have somewhere to go, the street side of the building is raised on poured concrete piers. This space beneath the piers—I assume it was intended for human habitation—has matching poured concrete benches, which are about as *gemütlich* as an underground parking garage, the thing it resembles most closely. I pass by on numerous occasions at the beginning of June, when the weather is fine and the campus is full of alumni, but no one is sitting there. Perhaps it is all that reinforced concrete overhead, lending an air of menace to the space underneath the building. Perhaps it is the sense of wasted space that the ramps and pilings inevitably create. No one wants to put in time in wasted space. Wasted space gives one a sense of wasted human resources, and one likes to consider oneself as valuable—infinitely valuable, as a matter of fact—and not something to be parked somewhere. So why should one want to occupy space in what looks like an underground parking garage?

Two painters who are working on the Fogg Museum's window frames sit on a wall that divides the underground sitting area from the street and eat their lunch. They avoid the concrete benches under the ramps.

"Let's face it", said the acting librarian at the Loeb Library in the basement of the new Graduate School of Design at Harvard (designed by John Andrews, M. Arch., Harvard, 1958), "the building just doesn't work." The new Graduate School of Design building is a poured-concrete affair, like Mather House. As with so many buildings of this sort, one doesn't have a clear sense of outside giving way to inside when one enters. That's because inside and outside were no longer supposed to be seen as antithetical, much less antagonistic. Everything now was to be "open". The Graduate School of Design was originally designed to be an "open building", like "atonal music", one of the many artistic oxymorons of the twentieth century. The entryway, the librarian tells me, was originally intended to be just like a street. The building was to have numerous doors, which were to be open twenty-four hours a day. Then, shortly after the building was opened, things started getting stolen, and the various doors began to be locked. Once again sixties philosophy did not correspond to sixties practice. Openness here as in other classrooms simply meant that those without scruples tyrannized those who were trying to work.

According to the original design, books were to be distributed throughout the building in various "pods", a scheme that proved to be a nightmare for the librarians as well as anyone trying to find a particular book.

As a result the librarians put their collective foot down and insisted on a
library, "which is why we were put in the basement", she added. The
basement originally had no windows, but its offices did have glass walls,
again as a tribute to openness. The librarians insisted again, and windows
were installed just above ground level in the north wall. The University
had to spend more than one million dollars trying to get the heat right,
still without success. In the winter, the library offices are so cold that the
employees have to wear fingerless gloves—*à la* Bob Cratchit—to keep
their hands warm.

On the other hand, the so-called "trays", the studios where the students
do their work, heat up like an oven because of their peculiar construction.
In keeping with the "open" design of the building in general, they are a
multilevel open area on the east side of the building, which is completely
under glass. The trays are like the grandstands of a stadium that isn't
there—all covered in glass. Once they are assigned to their particular
"tray", the students invariably erect cubicles of wallboard to ward off the
agoraphobia this structure inspires. On the day of the reception following
that year's graduation, two women students were in their trays clearing
out their things. When I mentioned the wallboard still in evidence, they
said that during the school year there was normally a lot more up. The
students felt compelled to fight back against the "openness" by building
not only walls but ceilings as well. It was a bit like a Brazilian favela
erected in a multi-million dollar building—which is to say, disconcerting.
The walls and ceilings were necessary because it was impossible to concentrate without them. "It was a sixties building", sneered one of the students. "Everyone is into everyone else's business." "All sharing and
collaboration", sneered the other, to show she meant the terms sarcasti-
cally. "You all got to copy off each other", said a man who was helping to
move things.

The GSD is much like Crown Hall at IIT (fig. 33), the building that
Mies van der Rohe felt was his greatest achievement, first of all because
they are both house schools of architecture and design, but also because in
both you get the sense that the practical purpose of the building has been
contravened by an ideology that is trying to make some point at cross purposes with what a school building is supposed to be. Crown Hall is one
enormous glass-enclosed rectangular room, 120 feet by 220 feet in plan
and 18 feet in height. There is not one supporting pillar in this huge interior space, all support in the building coming from four pairs of wide flange
columns supporting a plate girder roof. Crown Hall is, in other words,
one big room. Mies van der Rohe felt that such a space was the ideal setting for teaching the modern art of *Baukunst*—as opposed to architecture.

Figure 31.
Peabody Terrace, Harvard
University, Charles River
in foreground

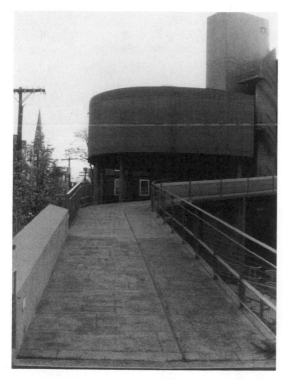

Figure 32.
The Carpenter Center for
the Visual Arts, Harvard
University

Figure 33. Crown Hall, Illinois Institute of Technology, interior

Figure 34. Crown Hall, Illinois Institute of Technology, exterior

"As a shared space", Franz Schulze writes in his biography of Mies van der Rohe,

> it implied shared goals and methods held in common by its users, shared values. . . . Crown Hall was "the clearest structure we have done, the best to express our philosophy", as Mies himself put it in his familiar, quasi-papal first person plural.[1]

Unfortunately all of those values being shared in one large stone-floored room created considerable distractions for anyone who was trying to concentrate on his own work. Schulze goes on to admit that Crown Hall, in spite of its philosophical purity, did have a number of practical drawbacks. Certain "practical inconveniences attended its use . . . noise, for example, from one class or project might interfere with the concentration of another a few feet away".[2] It is a strange and damning admission from a school whose main dogma was that "form was to follow function". However, by the time the Bauhausler got to America they had become—to use Tom Wolfe's phrase—"great white gods", and the buildings they built had more religious significance than they did practicality.

The Carman Hall Apartments (fig. 35) on the IIT campus, designed by Mies van der Rohe in 1951, is a thoroughly unpleasant building, unpleasant to look at with its peeling concrete piers and shoddy factory look and even more unpleasant to be in. The corridors are narrow, and the one-room apartment I visited on this warm summer day is suffocatingly hot. There is no cross-ventilation, and the one room faces a wall of glass of which only three panes open—three hopper windows that open out at less than a forty-five-degree angle, allowing virtually no air into the room. The building superintendent tells me that those who live there can have air-conditioners installed, but they must first have special hoods attached to the inside of the window, so as not to destroy the aesthetic unity of the building—a building that looks indistinguishable from any number of factories on the South Side. Total cost of installing one air-conditioner in one of these so-called "functional" buildings was three hundred dollars, not counting the cost of the air-conditioner itself. The tenant had to pay seventy-five dollars; the rest was subsidized by the university in the interest of "aesthetic unity".

Like Carman Hall Apartments at IIT, Harkness Commons at Harvard (fig. 36, 37) is classic Bauhaus workers' housing. Designed by Gropius himself, or the TAC (The Architect's Cooperative), his Cambridge firm, it

---

[1] Schulze, *Mies van der Rohe*, p. 263.
[2] Ibid.

Figure 35.
Carmen Hall, Illinois Institute
of Technology

Figure 36.
Harkness Commons,
Harvard University

Figure 37.
Harkness Commons,
Harvard University

is a loose assembly of three- or four-story square apartment buildings of beige brick with aluminum window frames and lots of plate glass. According to Probst and Schädlich, Harkness Commons broke the pattern of traditional architecture at Harvard. Aside from Gropius' house in Lincoln, Massachusetts, it was this country's first modern building. The two huge plate-glass windows in the dining hall look out at a stainless steel sculpture called "Tree of Life". It looks like a combination TV antenna and one of those umbrella-like poles you fix in the ground to dry clothes on. Either that or a very dangerous set of monkey bars.

The concrete on the balconies is starting to crumble, and the flat roof at the end of one of the walkways connecting the buildings is rust-stained and dripping little calcium stalactites around the run-off spout, showing unmistakable signs that the flat roof, in spite of everything that Gropius said to the contrary, does in fact leak. He insisted that the one on his house in Lincoln didn't in an article he did for *House and Garden* in 1949, leading one to suspect that it had become a sensitive issue with him. The flat roof was an article of faith for the Bauhausler, one whose religious dimensions would be exposed if the flat roof indeed did leak, which, as everyone knows, it indeed does. Once the impracticality of the flat roof becomes apparent, its antitranscendental meaning becomes obvious. When it comes to modern architecture, the flat roof is a non-negotiable item. There were only two requirements for collaborating on the *Weissenhofsiedlung* in Stuttgart; the building had to be white, and it had to have a flat roof. As Isaacs says, after Gropius lost a commission for a complex of sixteen hundred apartment units because he insisted on building them with flat roofs: "He would rather give up a job than compromise his principles" (520). The flat roof provides a direct and frontal confrontation with the heavens and not the rapprochement of the peaked roof—a rapprochement that reaches its pinnacle, in a manner of speaking, in the church steeple, which tapers off to nothing as its way of meeting the infinite, the cross being the point of mediation. Gropius, the twentieth-century avatar of socialism in stone, in this respect is like Johann von Leyden, who insisted that church steeples be torn down in Muenster in order to create the same sort of roof-top egalitarianism.

Gropius mentions in his piece on collegiate architecture that he saw the quadrangle of space surrounded by buildings as typical of Harvard, the best-known example being Harvard Yard. But the most beautiful example of that architectural form is the Georgian village that is the Harvard Business School on the Boston side of the Charles River. The Graduate School of Business (fig. 39) was built mostly in 1926 by the firm of McKim, Mead, White. The people who gave Mather House to Harvard

(Shepley, Bulfinch, Richardson, and Abbott) built a Bauhaus-inspired addition, Baker Hall, in 1968, but it is just as inspired by the desire to remain in the general style of business-school Georgian. Gropius at one point referred to the business school as "beautiful" but sneeringly referred to the project of doing it at some point other than in the 18th century as "archaeological" renovation. One gets the sense that the business school was some sort of silent reproach that stuck in Gropius' mind: "Our contemporary architectural conception of an intensified outdoor-indoor relation through wide window openings and large, undivided window panes has ousted the small, cage-like 'Georgian' window." [3] Cage-like? It is a curious phrase. It reminds one of the fact that the only other architectural renovation Gropius achieved at Harvard was the enlarged windows he built into the otherwise traditional Boylston Hall. Because the new windows are so large they expose stairwell and floors and all sorts of supporting elements in the most awkward manner. In the upper floor at the top of the multi-story windows, the light comes into the room at knee-level.

Gropius' attitude toward the Harvard Business School calls to mind one of Picasso's attempts late in life to exorcise the tradition of Western art by repeatedly copying (and thereby mutilating) works of the masters who had preceded him. Standing in the midst of the Harkness buildings, one suspects that Gropius had the business school in mind, with its arches and ivy-covered brick walls and paths that pique the curiosity of a person walking along them. Walking along Kennedy Avenue and looking into one of those arches, one senses that pleasant surprises await along that particular path. And, indeed, one is not disappointed; for the courts of the business school are one pleasant surprise after another. Perhaps it's the combination of red-brick Georgian arch framed by yew and ivy and rhododendron and azaleas, blooming just in time for the alumni gatherings. One has the sense of being let into an enclosed garden, which is one of the images for the Blessed Virgin in the Litany of Loreto. It is like the embrace of a chaste woman. Bauhaus, on the other hand, is like sodomy in the bushes of Buena Vista Park. Or, to be more precise historically, adultery on the Orient Express.

So the archways—actually, the flat metal overhangs—of Harkness Commons are not so much an imitation of the arches at the business school as a parody thereof. They are a bit like saying marriage and adultery are the same thing—which is to say, they are simultaneously parody and violation. One end of one of the Harkness buildings (fig. 40) is, as one has come to expect, supported on concrete pillars, under which one finds completely

[3] Gropius, "Twentieth Century Collegiate Architecture".

Figure 38. The Business School,
Harvard University

Figure 39. The Business
School, Harvard University

Figure 40. Harkness Commons,
Harvard University

Figure 41. Harkness Commons,
Harvard University

dead space, now occupied by bicycle racks with rusted junk bicycles chained to them with rusted locks left there by students who have probably long since graduated. If one has a decent bicycle in Cambridge, one takes it inside at night. The Cambridge Bicycle Shop takes its composite frame megabuck bike out of the show window in the evening lest some cycling enthusiast with a brick in his hand and few scruples gets ideas. The view from the bike racks under the overhang and through the concrete pilings to the easternmost building of the complex, which at the end of the day is baked in the setting sun, is like socialism's view of the future, which is to say, intolerable. There is nothing but flatness confronting flatness, the flat roof affronting the cloudless sky in some sort of silent confrontation. The mind hopes desperately for some sort of tree as mediation, anything but that bleak confrontation of building and infinity which Edward Hopper captured so well in his paintings.

The flat roof is the socialists' negation of God, and without God there is no future. Which is precisely the feeling one gets. All the emphasis on city planning that Gropius made throughout his life—the speech he gave praising the communists in Leningrad in 1933 is a good example—is the socialists' way of playing God. The vistas as a result give one the feelings of agoraphobia and hopelessness—no future—something like the way Reinhold Meissner felt when he crossed Antarctica on foot. One gets the sense that the future will be just like the past, that nothing is going to change. Unlike the Georgian arches of the Business School, which encourage exploration by promising some pleasing contact with nature, sort of an analogue to the situation of America in the eighteenth century, the socialist vista blocks out nature, nature's God, and the time-based fecundity based on the interaction of those things with man. Is that why the sundial is such a prominent feature of Georgian gardens? The sundial is the Puritan equivalent of the fountain, which one finds at the center of Italian gardens. Puritan culture was not as sensual as the Italian—read Nathaniel Hawthorne's *The Marble Faun* for a good analysis of the confrontation between the two—but at least it admits the existence of God in its way.

But that faith in God has disappeared completely from the Bauhaus universe, to be replaced by "Faith in Planning" (to use the words Gropius used as the title of a speech he gave while at Harvard). The planned city never really caught on in the United States—unless you want to see Levittown (Gropius abhorred it) as an example. To find it in its purest form you have to go to the suburbs of Moscow. It is the expression in concrete of those who want to live in the future because they really don't believe that a future—as the locus of time coming from God—really exists. The response of the people who have been quartered there by the State is the feeling that there is not much point in working since everything has been (to use a common phrase) taken care of. So the most appropriate response to the vision of the future presented by the blank façade of Bauhaus workers' housing is the decision to go out and get drunk or smoke crack.

Once the sun hits the windows of Harkness Commons, the rooms heat up very quickly. Because there is no cross ventilation in the rooms—in contradiction to all that Gropius said in his writings on worker housing in the twenties and thirties—one must open the door of the apartment in order to get fresh air. In order to get fresh air, one has to violate one's sense of privacy. This procedure is further necessitated by the fact that the windows don't open properly either. They are smudgy hatch-like affairs in their obligatory aluminum frames, opening outward from the bottom only to about fifteen degrees. Ninety percent of whatever breeze is blowing bounces off the window even when it has been opened. Consider further that the buildings of Harkness are considerably closer together than those of the yard, so not as much air gets in there in the first place, and you have a situation not particularly pleasant. An Iranian student entering the building says that he finds the building disappointing—it reminds him of his stay in China. "It's very socialistic", he says.

Figure 42. Ise Gropius, 1924

Chapter 13

BAUHAUS WEIMAR

October 1923

By 1923, Walter Gropius seems to have tired of juggling so many women.
In May of that year he met Ilse Frank, the twenty-six-year-old employee
of a book store in Hanover that specialized in writings of the avant-garde.
Shortly thereafter, Miss Frank told Gropius that she thought she was pregnant. On October 16, 1923, the two were married in a civil ceremony
with Paul Klee and Wassily Kandinsky as witnesses. Isaacs informs us that
"neither Walter nor Ise [as she was called now; he had persuaded her to
modify her name] put much stock in a church wedding" (313).

After the wedding he had to take some time to straighten out his affairs,
so to speak. The most pressing, of course, was the one with Lily Hildebrandt, who was completely in the dark concerning the new rival from
Hanover. Isaacs does not mention how Gropius broke the news to Lily. It
must have been an interesting letter, though. The man who described
himself as a "free spirit" after his divorce with Alma, as well as a "shooting
star in the firmament and extravagantly involved with the opposite sex",
now had to explain why he had chosen to bind himself in marriage once
again. Isaacs says only that Gropius' conscience bothered him when he
wrote to Lily, but that eventually the relationship spun itself into something "purely platonic" (318). He also never missed a chance to inquire
about Mrs. Hildebrandt's health, we are told. Earlier in the relationship
Lily apparently held Gropius responsible for an illness she contracted. Gropius, however, vehemently denied responsibility. Isaacs doesn't say specifically, but it seems as if Lily is referring to a venereal disease (279).

Gropius let his young bride take care of one of the other women in his
life, Frau Felleher. Gropius had met Mrs. Felleher, an artist married to a
famous painter, in Ascona shortly after he had begun his affair with Lily
Hildebrandt. An affair followed, which evidently Mrs. Felleher took more
seriously than Gropius did. She refused to give up on Gropius and continued to write him letters long after she knew that he had married Ise. As his
way out of an uncomfortable situation, Gropius gave Mrs. Felleher's letters
to his wife and asked her to take care of them: "This sad letter from Fel-

leher [he refers to her with the use of the definite article—*die Felleher*—
which is derogatory in German usage] came today", he writes to Ise. "I
feel sorry for her. Please write her a few words and then give the letter
back to me. I'm not going to send her a picture, since you don't want me
to" (318). Ise and Walter, Isaacs tells us, used to run into Frau Felleher in
Ascona in later years when they went there on vacation. There were to be
other women and other outbursts of jealous anger as well, but Gropius
seems to have handled them all without too much public scandal.

Bauhaus Weimar was having its problems, however, and these were not
totally unrelated to the private lives of the director and the teachers there.
The state-wide elections in Thuringia in 1924 drove the Social Democrats
out of power, and in their place a coalition of right-wing parties formed a
government, which brought about a turning point in the fate of the
school. According to Isaacs:

> Opponents of the Bauhaus, representatives of the craftsmen, and proponents
> from the old school of fine arts exploited the indecisive and contradictory
> position of government functionaries and pushed for a closing of the school.
> The reasons they dragged out were various: one spoke of increasing com-
> munist subversion, of a threat to the existence of private crafts and trades, of
> the squandering of public money, of immorality among students and teach-
> ers, and anything else one could dig up (577).

All in all it was the sort of behavior one has come to expect of art students, but it must have seemed new to the German authorities at the time.
Isaacs tries to dismiss the charge with sarcasm, but he provides very little
evidence that the charges weren't true. The one charge he bothers to re-
fute was the charge of squandering public money, which was a complicated issue because the inflation raging in Germany at the time made any
type of financial calculation virtually impossible. Contracts doubled in cost
overnight. A delay in buying an item from morning to evening effectively
doubled its cost. Gropius struggled through this period as best he could—
often selling off his own property and art work, frequently through Lily
Hildebrandt's husband—as a way of financing the school. Gropius most
certainly did not get rich at the public trough from Bauhaus.

But what about the other charges? Gropius maintained vociferously that
there was nothing political about the Bauhaus; however, his denials are either semantic or disingenuous to the point of dishonesty, depending on
how we look at them. When Gropius maintained that Bauhaus was apolitical, he was referring to party politics. He wanted Bauhaus to have nothing to do with either the Nazis or the communists. However, he was
deeply allied with the Social Democrats, and when the political situation

Figure 43. Conflict between Bauhaus and the city of Dessau, 1928

changed in Weimar, he moved Bauhaus to Dessau because the Social Democrats were in power there. Even Gropius' overtly Marxist hand-picked successor, Hannes Meyer, made the same sort of distinction. Meyer assured the increasingly suspicious Social Democrat mayor of Dessau that "my activity has always been aimed at the politics of culture, never of parties" (*nur kulturpolitisch, niemals parteipolitisch*) (581). But that was precisely the point. Bauhaus was a socialistic alternative to the whole idea of society being run by political parties. It was, to coin a phrase, politics by design. It was, to use the phrase of its opponents, "*Kulturbolschewismus*", of precisely the sort practiced now by countries such as the United States through such agencies as the National Endowment for the Arts. As Bruno Taut, another proponent of *das neue Wohnen*, wrote in 1919, it was "socialism in the unpolitical, superpolitical sense of the word, alien to each and every form of hegemony; as the simple relation of one man to another it transcends warring social classes and nations and binds one man to another" (398).

Nothing stands still, however, and by the 1930s, Bauhaus had become quite undeniably the communist cell that Gropius had denied it was when under his own direction. When Hannes Meyer was forced out as director, with Gropius' collaboration, he turned his back on Germany and emigrated to Moscow. Before leaving, he gave a little farewell address in which he said that he was "moving to the Soviet Union in order to work in a place where a genuine proletarian culture was being forged, where socialism was being born, where the society exists for which we're fighting here under capitalism" (581–82). Gropius wanted to be a revolutionary in his own way. When Meyer became overtly communist, Gropius turned on him, apparently feeling that the apolitical alternative was the more successful over the long run. Today, it is easy to see that he was right. Bolshevism may have gone out of style in the lands of Eastern Europe, but its cultural variant is still the reigning orthodoxy among the universities and media and publishing houses and government granting agencies of the West.

But beyond semantics, there is evidence that Gropius was being just plain dishonest about his intentions. In late December of 1919, he was writing to Lily Hildebrandt that Bauhaus Weimar was "the beginning of the European cultural revolution" (235). On July 9, 1920, however, Gropius appeared before the state assembly—to ask for state money, of course—and assured the assembled state representatives that he would prove to them that "Bauhaus was a development and not a tearing down of tradition" (244).

As to the charge that Bauhaus was involved in the "corruption of morals", there is, as we have seen, a good deal of substantiation of that charge in the life of Gropius himself. One of his affairs, after all, was with one of his Bauhaus students. Beyond that, though, we are not just talking about a weakness that contradicted principles. Those who display such weakness are vulnerable to the charge of hypocrisy, but hypocrisy can also be seen as the tribute vice pays to virtue. We are talking instead about an ideology, not so much a weakness at odds with principle as an attack on principle itself as the outcome of rationalized misbehavior.

Those who wield the sword of revolution should also recognize that it has a double edge. Gropius took his young wife to Weimar and then to

Figure 44. Gropius in Italy, 1924

Dessau, and he schooled her in the philosophy of Bauhaus, only to find out that she was a more apt pupil than he suspected.

In the summer of 1930, Ise Gropius was spending time at the Casa Hausler in Ascona, a mountain resort on Lake Maggiore in southeastern Switzerland, with a number of other members of the "Bauhaus family", as she termed it. The phrase itself should have tipped Gropius off that something was going on behind his back—again. But as Isaacs says, he was "the last one to know" (602). Ise had fallen in love with a younger man, someone her own age. Isaacs does not tell us his name, but we know from the correspondence that he was an old friend and a member of the "Bauhaus family". Some family.

Figure 45. Gropius' office, Bauhaus Weimar, 1923

"I know how you feel", Gropius was to say when Ise told him the truth about her affair. "I did the same thing myself once" (602). Well, not exactly once, at least twice, as a matter of fact, but now Gropius was in the role that Gustav Mahler had played some twenty years earlier. Ise, for her part, was playing Alma's role in a strange sort of way, too. According to her own words, Ise "adored the idea of being in love, in the mountains, along with the skiing". When Gropius reproached her for her infidelity, she responded by saying that she now considered herself "irrevocably married to the Bauhaus idea of the family and its fate" (610). As a counterproposal, she asked for his permission to spend the next four weeks in the mountains with her lover. "Will you give your approval to our love affair?" (610) Ise wanted to know. Gropius surely was no stranger himself to the "Bauhaus idea of the family". Because of that and the fact that he was politically astute, he made a virtue of necessity and said she could spend two weeks with him instead of four. The incident has eerie resonances not only with Gropius cuckolding Gustav Mahler (now Gropius was at the other end of the knife, so to speak) but also with the suggestion that Alma Mahler made that he and Werfel could share her for six months of the year, respectively. However, Mahler put his family life on the line by forcing Alma to choose. Even the invariably sympathetic Isaacs finds Gropius' acquiescence in the matter off-putting. He concludes the episode by saying that there was no repeat of this particular sort of "family" experiment, but that the affair continued nonetheless.

Figure 46. Farnsworth House, Plano, Illinois

Chapter 14

PLANO, ILLINOIS

Summer 1990

Farnsworth House is in many ways the apotheosis of Bauhaus philosophy. It is a glass box on stilts five feet above the ground on the flood plain of the Fox River, some fifty miles west of Chicago. It was designed by Mies van der Rohe in the early fifties, when Bauhaus architecture had reached its peak of influence.

The career of Ludwig Mies van der Rohe recapitulates that of Walter Gropius in a minor key. Born Ludwig Mies (he added the Dutch and faintly aristocratic sounding "van der Rohe" when he married above himself in Berlin), the son of a stone carver in Aachen, Mies moved to the architectural offices of Peter Behrens just as Gropius was leaving to start his own firm. Mies married a woman of independent means in the second decade of this century and designed a series of perfectly conventional houses for the wealthy bourgeois who were now part of his circle. (In this sense Gropius antedated him in ideas, but Mies was to aver that Gropius couldn't draw—a charge that Gropius himself admitted, hence the constant note of collaboration in his work. From Adolf Meyer to the TAC in Cambridge, Gropius was an idea man.) Throughout the teen years of this century, Mies played the part of the conventionally married man and designed conventional houses. His wife, who seemed determined to overlook his infidelities because of his stature as "the artist", bore him three daughters. Back in Berlin after World War I, Mies attached himself to the avant-garde of the time and promptly abandoned his wife and children. It was at precisely this moment that he began designing what are clearly recognizable as "modern" buildings, his unbuilt "glass skyscraper" of 1922 being a good example.

Mies never divorced his first wife—to have done so would have cut him off from an important source of funds. But from that moment on, his domestic life was that of a man who had one affair after another—the more long-lasting were with Lily Reich in Germany and Lora Marx in the United States. However, he still chose to live alone. One of his later conquests was a tall, unattractive Chicago nephrologist by the name of Edith

Farnsworth. She met Mies at the home of a mutual friend in 1945, and by the end of that year she had commissioned him to build a house for her. Considering the auspices under which it began, it is not surprising that the relationship ended in rancor.

Mies worked on the design and construction of Farnsworth House from 1946 to 1951. In the end he had to initiate a lawsuit to get paid—but the lawsuit proved to be a pyrrhic victory. Farnsworth's lawyer, Randolph Bohrer, says of Mies' testimony in court: "You can't believe what an exhibition of ignorance he put on! He didn't know anything about steel, its properties or its standard dimensions. Nor about construction or high school physics or just plain common sense. All he knows is that guff about his concept and in the Kendall County Courthouse that doesn't go down. I tell you, we had him sweating blood—he was heard to say afterwards that he would never start another lawsuit." [1]

But by the summer of 1953, neither Mies' ignorance of the properties of steel nor Gropius' inability to draw meant much to a world that had converted to their philosophy of life. Bauhaus had arrived. The Bauhausler had the good fortune to be attacked by the Nazis in the 1930s and then to reap the benefits of that attack twenty years later, especially in Germany, where building in the Bauhaus style became an act of public expiation, similar to monetary compensation paid to Jews and Gypsies. Now that it had arrived, the philosophy that said form followed function didn't have to make sense as architecture any more. It could become the pure architectural expression of the modernist credo. It could become ideology in glass and concrete.

Farnsworth House is an aggressive expression of the secular horizontality of the modern age. Its flat roof confronts the sky in silent and implacable opposition; its floor hangs suspended five feet above the earth, disdaining any contact with it, the objective correlative of the deracination to which moderns aspired. As at Carpenter Hall at Harvard, one is struck by how effectively this building kills the space beneath it. One of the prominently visible features of Farnsworth House, when one approaches it on foot, is the dead space beneath it. Under the house there is a large expanse of—well, brown dirt. The house is a bit like an alien spaceship whose retro thrusters destroyed with their heat everything below it upon landing; but, at the same time, it remains perched above the ground as if ready to blast off at a moment's notice. Farnsworth House sits five feet above the soil of Illinois as if full of disdain at settling down onto the earth in any sustained relationship. In this it was much like Mies' attitude toward America and toward Marx.

---

[1] Schulze, *Mies van der Rohe*, p. 258.

"Tell me", Lora Marx, his American lover, once asked him, "why you never married me."

"I think I was a fool", Mies replied. "I was afraid I would lose my freedom. I wouldn't have. It was a senseless worry."

Then as if of a mind to make up for past mistakes, Mies asked her if she would marry him.

"No", was Marx's answer. She died in 1966 of cancer of the esophagus. Mies died three years later in the summer of 1969, just weeks after the death of Walter Gropius.[2]

One can imagine what Farnsworth House would look like were it put in the service of conventional domesticity, i.e., one involving children. The carefully raked Illinois soil underneath it would quickly become cluttered with broken tricycles, a dog on its chain along with its food bowl, and all of the other paraphernalia of family life on this planet. But even without all that, one is struck by the expanse of dirt under the house, which, even with being kept free of the evidence of domesticity, has all the appeal of a failed mushroom farm.

Farnsworth House is the epitome of the International Style at its most frankly utopian. In between the affront to the heavens and the disdaining of the earth, there are four plate-glass walls—in other words nothing, or, as Mies himself would say, "practically nothing" (*beinahe Nichts*). It was a phrase he liked, one that Frank Lloyd Wright parodied in a letter to Mies. Domestic life was to take place in this frankly utopian arrangement, rooted neither in the earth nor in heaven, with virtually no privacy, with no barriers between the home and the outside world.

Perhaps as a compensation for the agoraphobia that Farnsworth House induces in its inhabitants, the current owner has installed floor-to-ceiling draperies to close off every square inch of glass from the outside. Visitors are confronted by a wall of beige curtain, broken by two cricket bats and a slight opening at the door, through which one can peer, voyeur-like, into the house's interior. In addition to adding the draperies, the owner has planted a number of maple saplings along the riverbank, making the house invisible from the river and the state park across it, but also rendering the river invisible from inside the house. Like the devotée who refuses to give up a fanatical ideology, the owner of Farnsworth House must involve himself in self-contradiction in order to make living there humanly possible. The draperies, the saplings, and the black chainlink fence topped with barbed wire surrounding the entire property are eloquent testimony that a *home* necessitates the distinction between inside

---

[2] Ibid., p. 132.

and outside, which the architecture of the house so confidently contradicts.

Privacy, when driven out of architecture, takes up its abode in furnishings, landscaping, and fence construction. All of this must be done in order to ensure that domestic life is possible. Of course, the net result is that one is cut off from the environment in a radical way, a way that would not have been necessary if the canons of traditional architecture had been applied instead. The throwing down of the rules of social discourse necessitates other, more extravagant means of control. Farnsworth House is to architecture what nudism is to social gathering. Once the most obvious barriers are dropped, all sorts of ancillary rules must be adopted to ensure that the normal activities of life don't degenerate into chaos.

Looked at another way, Farnsworth House was Mies' way of ensuring that domestic life would be impossible. The apotheosis of modern architecture was not the skyscraper, which the Americans had already invented; it was the creation of the anti-home, the *Wohnmaschine*. "The problem of the house", Le Corbusier said in *Towards a New Architecture* (right after he had defined the house as a "machine for living in")

> is a problem of the epoch. The equilibrium of society today depends upon it. Architecture has for its first duty, in this period of renewal, that of bringing about a revision of values, a revision of the constituent elements of the house.[3]

No one succeeded at Le Corbusier's challenge better than Mies did in the building of Farnsworth House. Of course, Mies was involved in a no-win situation here, for the more he succeeded in approaching the apotheosis of Bauhaus architectural ideology the more his buildings failed as architecture, a fact now evident even to Bauhaus' admirers. Franz Schulze, for example, in his biography of Mies, admits that

> certainly the [Farnsworth] house is more nearly a temple than a dwelling, and it rewards aesthetic contemplation before it fulfills domestic necessity. Mies's technology, in fact, often proved unequal to it in a strictly material sense. In cold weather the great glass panes tended to accumulate an overabundance of condensation, due to an imbalance in the heating system. In summer, despite the protection afforded by a glorious black sugar maple just outside the south wall, the sun turned the interior into a cooker. The cross ventilation [Schulze is referring to the building's three openings: a "portal" on the west side and two hopper windows on the east] availed little and the draperies which could be drawn along the walls were hardly more effective

---

[3] Le Corbusier, *Towards a New Architecture*, p. 12.

Figure 47. Farnsworth House, Plano, Illinois

Figure 48. Farnsworth House, Plano, Illinois

in reducing the interior heat. Mies rejected the idea of a screen covering for the door, and it was only his painful experience with the river valley mosquitoes that caused him to yield to Farnsworth's demand for a track on the ceiling of the patio, from which screens could be hung, thus permitting comfortable outdoor sitting. Peter Palumbo, the London real estate developer who purchased the house from Farnsworth in 1962, and who confesses to a reverence for Mies's architecture, has accepted the master's will: he removed the screens and, during hot summer days, leaves the door and windows open, putting up uncomplainingly with the insect life that finds its way into the house.[4]

Fiat voluntas tua. "Thy will be done" is the proper attitude of a client to architects who considered themselves gods. Palumbo, according to Schulze,

> is the ideal owner of this house. He is wealthy enough to maintain it with the infinite and eternal care it requires, and he lives in it for only short periods during any given year. Thus he finds it easier to do what anyone must who chooses to reside there: he derives sufficient spiritual sustenance from the reductivist beauty of the place to endure its creature discomforts.[5]

So it turns out that Gropius was right after all: Bauhaus was a religion and, as the devotion of Peter Palumbo shows, a particularly demanding one at that. The house that was to epitomize the utilitarian credo can be inhabited only for a short period of time during the year. Otherwise one is overcome by the mosquitos and the heat. In the winter, contemplation is less fraught with physical discomfort, but the condensation on the windows tends to obscure the view. But what exactly does one contemplate in this house? What exactly does all this glass reveal?

[4] Schulze, *Mies van der Rohe*, p. 256.
[5] Ibid.

Chapter 15

GROPIUS HOUSE, LINCOLN, MASSACHUSETTS

June 1990

The woman who is leading the tour of the house that Gropius built here in 1937, right after he arrived in the United States to take up his professorship at Harvard, is a little nervous this Saturday morning. A small crowd has arrived in time for the noonday tour conducted by the Society for the Preservation of New England Antiquities, and this is her first time on the job.

Gropius House sits about one hundred yards off Baker Bridge Road on a slight hill behind a low stone wall and a few trees, at the end of a gently upward-sloping driveway ending in a small, gravel parking lot. If one continues on Baker Bridge Road out of Lincoln, one comes to Walden Pond, which was famous for a house of another, more modest, but equally metaphysical sort. Beyond Walden Pond, there is the house that Hawthorne rented from Emerson, in which he wrote *Mosses from an Old Manse*. And beyond that, there is the bridge across which someone fired the shot heard round the world, the one that began a revolution in 1776. It is a region full of historic buildings.

"The first thing you should notice", says the nervous lady leading the tour, "is how well the house fits in with its local surroundings." Dutifully, we all look at the house and then at the surroundings, and I conclude that it fits into the New England landscape about as well as a spaceship from Mars would. In fact, in comparison with the other houses in the area, it looks like just that—a spaceship that has landed on a hill and disgorged an army of alien invaders. It was built near the time Orson Welles did his "War of the Worlds" spoof on the radio and is in many ways similar—except that this is the real thing. This was the first *Wohnmaschine* to land on the North American continent. From this idyllic point, so rich in the history of this nation, the alien invaders spread out to conquer our cities, which they did within a matter of twenty-five years. In 1962, the world's cities awoke and groaned to find themselves Bauhausian.

"The house may not seem very special to you now," the nervous lady says after we move indoors, "but you have to realize that when it was built

119

Figure 49. Gropius House, Lincoln, Massachusetts

Figure 50.
Gropius House,
Lincoln, Massachusetts

it was very revolutionary." Now it looks, well, just mechanical. It reminds me of GE appliance ads of the sort one would find in *Life* magazine in the fifties. In fact, all of the appliance companies vied to get their wares into Gropius House so that they could market them later as part of the house of the future. Our guide makes us aware of the fact that virtually every-thing in the house—the windows and so forth—were taken from standard industrially designed materials available at the time, everything except the banister to the upstairs, which is black and snakes up oddly through the stairwell. The house has a typical inside–outside reversal so beloved of the Bauhausler. The outside is done in tongue-and-groove board, the inside in clapboard. "The house is enriched", I read in a brochure, "by humane touches that serve the needs of this particular family. Gropius recognized his twelve-year-old [adopted] daughter's growing need for privacy and de-signed her bedroom with its own sun porch and outside entrance via the spiral staircase" (fig. 50).

The most unusual-looking room in the house, though, is the master bedroom. It is bisected asymmetrically by a large plate-glass window, to allow (so the explanation goes) Walter and Ise to sleep where it was cool and dress where it was warm. The visual effect, however, reveals none of that. The plate-glass window reminds one of the display window in a de-partment store façade, the marital bed being the object under display.

The room is empty now. As with the Farnsworth House, you get the impression that the true meaning of the plate-glass goes beyond conven-tional explanations. It is a metaphysical statement about the family. It was Gropius' attempt to defeat the mystery of the home, the place where so many things went on behind his back, where he did so many things be-hind the backs of other men. It was an attempt to rationalize domesticity, to put it under glass and thereby conform it to the truncated philosophy of life that was modernity. In the end, though, this curiously designed bed-room, along with monuments such as the Farnsworth House, reveals nothing more than the transparency of its architect's designs.

WORKS CITED

Le Corbusier and Pierre Jenneret. *Oeuvres Complètes, 1910-1929*. Zürich: Les Editions Birsberger, 1960.

Le Corbusier. *Towards a New Architecture*. Translated by Frederick Etchells. London: The Architectural Press; New York: Frederick A. Praeger, 1927.

Gropius House. Society for the Preservation of New England Antiquities.

Isaacs, Reginald R. *Walter Gropius: Der Mensch und sein Werk*. Berlin: Gebr. Mann Verlag, 1983.

Jungk, Peter Stephan. *Franz Werfel: Eine Lebensgeschichte*. Frankfurt am Main: S. Fischer, 1987.

Monson, Karen. *Alma Mahler: Muse to Genius*. New York: Houghton Mifflin, 1983.

Schulze, Franz. *Mies van der Rohe: A Critical Biography*. Chicago and London: University of Chicago Press, 1985.

Wingler, Hans M. *Das Bauhaus: 1919-1933 Weimar Dessau Berlin*. Wiesbaden: Verlag Bebr. Rasch & Co. and M. DuMont Schauberg, 1962.

Wolfe, Tom. *From Bauhaus to Our House*. New York: Harper and Row, 1983.

INDEX